Kum Nye Relaxation

Body, mind, and senses join through
a process of inner alchemy.

Kum Nye Relaxation

Part 1: Theory, Preparation, Massage

Tarthang Tulku

Dharma Publishing

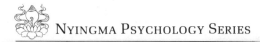 NYINGMA PSYCHOLOGY SERIES

Library of Congress Cataloging in Publication Data

Tarthang Tulku.
  Kum Nye relaxation.

  (Nyingma Psychology Series; 4)
  Includes index.
  1. Relaxation. 2. Mind and body. 3. Exercise.
4. Massage. I. Title.
RA785.T37   613.7'9   78-10418
ISBN 0–913546–10–0 (v. 1)
ISBN 0–913546–25–9 pbk. (v. 1)
ISBN 0–913546–75–5 (v. 2)
ISBN 0–913546–74–7 pbk. (v. 2)

Editing, illustration, and design by Dharma Publishing
Typeset in Fototronic Medallion, printed, and bound by
Dharma Press, California

9 8 7 6   *Printed in the USA*

Contents

Preface

Kum Nye relaxation is a gentle healing system which relieves stress, transforms negative patterns, helps us to be more balanced and healthy, and increases our enjoyment and appreciation of life. In these times when confusion and chaos are so much a part of daily activity, we are often too tense and charged up to enjoy life. Kum Nye opens our senses and our hearts so that we feel satisfied and fulfilled, and can appreciate more fully every aspect of our lives. Even in a short time, the quality of experience can be enriched, and our lives grow more harmonious.

The unique value of the Kum Nye system of relaxation is that it integrates and balances two approaches, the physical and the psychological. Kum Nye heals both our bodies and minds, bringing their energies together to function calmly and smoothly. Because it leads to the integration of body and mind in *all* our activities, this relaxation has a vital and lasting quality greater than the feeling of well-being experienced in physical exercise, or even in disciplines such as yoga. When we learn to open our senses and touch our feelings directly, our bodies and

minds make full contact with one another, and all our experience becomes richer, healthier, and more beautiful. As we become more deeply acquainted with ourselves and grow in self-understanding, we are also able to share more fully with others.

The written tradition of Kum Nye is contained in Tibetan medical texts, as well as in the ancient Vinaya texts of Buddhism. These texts deal with living according to physical and universal laws, and include extensive descriptions of healing practices. Kum Nye (which is pronounced Koom Nyay) is thus part of the lineage of spiritual and medical theories and practices which links Tibetan with Indian and Chinese medicine. This lineage has given rise to many disciplines, including yoga and acupuncture; it also forms the roots of many of the more recent body-mind disciplines.

Yet the system of Kum Nye presented here is thoroughly modern, drawn from my own experience, and adapted specifically to suit modern needs. When I was a young boy in Tibet, my father, a physician and a lama, introduced me to Kum Nye. Kum Nye, however, was not well known in Tibet, and was most often used as an adjunct to other practices. My gurus in the oral introductory yoga tradition of the *Nying-thig tsa-long* (subtle body energy system) sometimes taught the basic theory and practice of Kum Nye as an introductory practice. Kum Nye, however, has had no systematized body of written instructions until now, and my practice of Kum Nye had a flavor of exploration and experimentation.

I have used this open aspect of Kum Nye to make further adaptations. Over the past ten years, I have developed several hundred exercises which my Western students have found particularly helpful. These volumes include the simplest and most effective of these exercises, all of which can be done safely—by young and old—without a teacher. Breathing, self-massage, and different kinds of movement exercises are included. It is my hope that delight in the discovery of many as yet undeveloped aspects of

Kum Nye will enrich the practice of Western students, and eventually encourage systematization in Western terms.

I hope that this book will introduce the benefits of Kum Nye to many people of various backgrounds and interests, and will assist them in developing and continuing their experience of inner relaxation. I have intended the book to be a practical guide to the deep pleasure of a healthy and balanced life, rich in beauty and enjoyment, and leading to harmony for all beings, even in these difficult times.

I am very grateful to the many people whose experience of Kum Nye has contributed to the development of these exercises, and I dedicate this book to the Nyingma Institute in Berkeley, California, where Kum Nye blossomed in its present form.

Tarthang Tulku
September, 1978

Exercises and Massages

Stimulating Energies: Stage One

Stimulating Energies: Stage Two

Stimulating Energies: Stage Three

Kum Nye Relaxation

The Inner and Outer
Massage of Feeling

*Through relaxation
we discover a whole new
way of being.*

We all have memories of times when we felt particularly alive, when the world seemed fresh and
promising, like a flower garden on a bright spring
morning. Whatever the circumstances leading to
such a moment, there is suddenly a sensation of acute
vitality supported by the knowledge that all elements
are in absolute harmony. The air pulses with life. Our
bodies feel healthy and energetic, our minds clear
and confident. There is a lucent quality to our per-
ception. Every feature of the environment pleases our
senses: colors are especially vivid, sounds are melo-
dious, and odors fragrant. All aspects of the experience blend perfectly and there is a vibrant quality to
everything; the usual border between inner and outer
space becomes fluid. Nothing is fixed, and we feel
spacious and open. We act with perfect ease and
appropriateness.

The essence of this experience is balance, and
its offshoot is a deep feeling of nurturance and re-

freshment which extends far beyond the feeling we ordinarily call 'happiness'. Kum Nye is the art of developing this balance. Through relaxation we discover a whole new way of being, an open perspective which delights in the integration of body, mind, senses, feelings, and environment. We learn to appreciate the completely wholesome quality of *living* experience. The whole body becomes refreshed, as if showered within by pure spring water. Not only the physical body quickens, but the mind and all of the senses as well; sense impressions and thoughts come to life. A quality of relaxation informs every activity, even walking or eating. Our lives function smoothly, and we become healthy and balanced.

The key to both our internal integration and a balanced relationship with the world lies within our feelings and sensations. We can nurture and heal both our bodies and minds by touching our feelings deeply and expanding the flowing rhythms they bring to us, for they are linked to the vitality of the universe itself. Through relaxation, we awaken feelings which then expand and accumulate until we slowly become aware of a deep, interpenetrating field of energy, inside our body and beyond it. This energy can stimulate itself internally to sustain and nurture us in our daily lives, recycling sensation so we become sensitive and strong, and our sensations rich and powerful. Our minds become clearer as well, and we discover what it means to be balanced.

Our senses, feelings, and thoughts are integrated, and all of our relationships, actions, ideas, and movements are flowing and harmonious. Our awareness gives us the freedom to take charge of our lives, not in a forceful or grasping way, but with confidence. We then naturally do what is appropriate and beneficial, and function in a positive way in the world. We realize that ideas and actions which result in stability and happiness for ourselves contribute also to the harmony of the world around us.

When we sense the beauty of the world, it seems natural to live in harmony with the universe, to enjoy a mutually satisfying relationship like a mare and her foal. But somehow we have become estranged from this state of being. Though we speak of Mother Nature, we are like her adolescent children, struggling with our own identities at the cost of losing the warmth and gentleness we vaguely remember.

In early childhood, when our senses were more open, we may have experienced a greater sense of union with the universe, but as we grow, we learn to foster our personalities too intensely, deepening feelings of separation rather than the feelings of warmth and security our hearts desire. The pressures and complications of modern society make it difficult to do otherwise, for to be successful in business, in friendship, even in play, we are almost forced into competitive and stressful situations which develop feelings of alienation and anxiety. All our major undertakings, including school, raising a family, and becoming established in a career, involve complications and limitations we cannot seem to avoid.

Even when we try to open our lives, we may end up contracting our experience rather than expanding it. Our mental and physical activities seldom succeed in truly satisfying us, because we do not integrate the two. Not realizing the importance of integrating body and mind in *all* our activities, we emphasize mental achievement at the expense of feeling, or our physical body at the expense of the rich sensations within.

When we restrict our feelings and sensations, we prevent them from giving us the sustenance we need to be healthy and happy. Our senses may react to this constriction, and subtly urge us to open, but our 'rational' mind is in control of delicate sense impressions, and so we may not even hear their plea. Hungry for fulfillment, we begin to search outside ourselves, often racing restlessly from one source of enjoyment to another, as if there were a limited supply. We become captivated by the idea that satisfaction is 'out there' . . . if only we look, work, or play hard enough. We are drawn to exciting activities which seem to stimulate our minds and senses, but leave us still wanting more. The faster we run, the further we move away from true satisfaction, which remains within, behind the door of the senses.

Instead of opening this door, we may turn to drugs such as alcohol or the hallucinogens. We may even turn to the spiritual path, hoping at last to be truly nurtured, only to discover that here, too, we are still dissatisfied. We continue to expend our energies jumping from experience to experience, from thought to thought. We imagine what we would like to have happen, or remember what it was like before;

we make plans. Lost in daydreams, we may glimpse a moment of pleasure or a rich sensation, but we do not experience the full flavor of the contact; somehow it eludes us.

We may attempt to regain a feeling of wholeness by 'ownership' of our families and of property, trying in this way to control both nature and our lives. But such control is artificial and out of touch with the natural laws and cycles which govern our bodies and minds, as well as the world around us. We begin to feel closed in and unfulfilled. Unable to see that our own lack of balance might have been the cause, we find ourselves in unhealthy situations, wondering how we got there.

We may finally come to believe that it is impossible for us to perceive things more substantially or to open into deeper levels of experience. We do not realize that through neglect, our senses have toughened like an elephant's hide, diminishing the fullness of our sensory capacity. Until we gently soften this 'toughness' by developing the natural energies of our feelings and sensations, we cannot open to the full field of experience.

When we really *know* this, we can participate in the natural flow of the universe, for we understand that we depend on nature, and nature, indeed the whole universe, depends on us. The world will be balanced when we are balanced. We are naturally bonded to the world: the elements which make up the universe are within each of us. We carry this ancient lineage in our bodies, and we are reflected in our families, our society, and our planet. Every action we take, however small, affects the whole universe, just as every wave affects the shore.

We participate in infinitely complex and interdependent relationships with all of the many levels of existence, from subatomic to cosmic. Like other systems in the universe, we are a complete unit in ourselves, yet we are composed of many smaller units which are all interrelated and which also interrelate with the whole. In addition to the many systems which make up the physical body—skeletal, muscular, nervous, etc.—there is the psychological or emotional system as well as other subtle energy systems. The smooth functioning of each of these systems depends on the functioning of every other system in the body, while the state of the entire unit which we call the 'human being' is intimately related to the condition of the surrounding environment.

Our immediate environment is also related to every other environment on earth, and the earth is influenced by events in the far reaches of the universe. We are influenced by many forces, some of which we barely perceive or understand, and our actions and thoughts affect other systems, including microscopic worlds within our bodies.

When we acknowledge these interrelationships, we acknowledge the importance of creating harmony within ourselves. We realize that we have within us the resources we need to be both balanced and happy, for our bodies and minds are the vehicles for all our learning and growth.

By slowing down, relaxing, and gently opening our senses, we can learn to develop these resources;

we then discover that we can heal our bodies and minds with feeling channeled through the physical body. When we lessen the chronic tightness in our muscles and minds, we sensitize ourselves to subtle qualities of feeling and bring them alive to vigorous and fresh experience, enriching them so they grow like strong shoots.

As our mental and physical energies are vitalized and become integrated, these sensations become much more fertile and nurturing than ordinary sensations. Their nourishment frees us from the vibrating distraction of jumping thoughts and the wishing for what is always beyond our reach. We discover the naturally alert and flowing state of the body, mind, and energy, so we are able to find satisfaction within ourselves. As our bodies and minds become good friends, our muscles also work well together, free from superfluous muscle tension. We have the concentration necessary for full experience. Our relationships then become richer and deeper, harmonious rather than competitive, for we relate more sensitively to others as well as to ourselves.

In Kum Nye, there are various ways, including both stillness and movement, to stimulate the flow of feeling and energy which integrates body and mind. We begin by developing stillness of body, breath, and mind. Simply sitting still and relaxing gives us a chance to appreciate feelings of which we are normally unaware. This relaxation is then subtly aided by breathing through both nose and mouth so gently and evenly that we are hardly conscious of inhaling and exhaling at all, a way of breathing which allows us to contact the positive vitality of the throat center.

As the breath becomes calm and quiet, fewer distracting thoughts and images run through the mind, and the whole body comes alive. Our mental and bodily energies become refreshed and tranquil, like a clear forest pool. We discover a quality of feeling common to body, breath, and mind—a calm, clear, deepening quality—which soothes and 'massages' us deep within. As we relax more, the subtle level of this feeling opens like a lens, letting in more 'light' or energy and creating more comprehensive 'pictures' of experience.

To explore the qualities of this relaxation further, we add self-massage and the 'massage' of movement exercise to sitting and breathing. Usually we think of massage as something done for us, but the body can massage itself. Massage can involve our feelings and sensations, and our whole inner structure, as well as our outer shape and form. During massage, subtle feeling-tones or energies permeate and soothe our whole being, integrating the mental and the physical, relating feeling to form. These energies are like a vibrating, moving aura which runs through us and outward from us, and also surrounds us. We can learn to heal ourselves inwardly with these energies, and direct them to flow outwardly, harmonizing all aspects of our being. We can generate an inner sun radiating feelings which warm us and pervade everything around us.

While at first we stimulate the massage physically—by breathing, pressing and rubbing our bodies, moving slowly in certain ways, or producing and releasing tension—later we can initiate massage through feeling-tones alone. As relaxation deepens, we begin to feel directly the interconnections among breath, senses, body, and mind. The senses open new channels and dimensions of sensation, releasing joyful feelings which can be expanded and accumulated until we are aware of nothing else in the world. Every cell becomes suffused and saturated with positive feelings of wholeness and completion. Even between the muscles and tissues, we drink in these wonderful feelings.

When we truly use our senses, every part of the body becomes vibrantly alive and healthy—mentally and emotionally we become fully awake. We discover we can experience ecstatic beauty at every moment as if we were always hearing beautiful music or seeing the finest works of art. We are even capable of healing ourselves, for this relaxation quickens a feeling-tone that itself becomes a self-generating massage, a system of self-nurturance that can be further expanded and developed. This is the massage of Kum Nye.

The deeper and richer our experience of this self-operating massage becomes, the more it simply occurs naturally, vitalizing every sense, feeling, and activity of daily life. Expanding in space and time, subtle feeling-tones or energies activate massage outside as well as inside our bodies, harmonizing surrounding levels of existence. Feelings of love or the joy of laughter gently expand beyond the body, floating through space and time like softly falling snow. All of our senses expand in a subtle way which increases enjoyment.

When seeing, we lightly concentrate on an object so that we sense a fooling from its form. BY opening our eyes in this way, we invite an ecstatic interaction between subtle 'inner' and 'outer' energies. Seeing then becomes vision, a constant expression of a vital totality.

Food becomes an offering to the senses. When we learn to enjoy all the feeling-tones of tasting, distributing them throughout the body and beyond it, eating is truly a meeting of the senses with their object, a ceremonial act of appreciation.

We learn to contact and appreciate sound as well, feeling it fully in our bodies, using it to stimulate harmonious interactions between ourselves and the surrounding universe. As we allow soft music to relax and soothe us when we are tired, we activate feelings which can even heal us. When we speak, each sound is gentle, so there is no shocking or destructive quality to our communication.

The sweetness bred by fully exercising our senses can be expanded more and more each day. Without trying to possess it, without any fixed goal, almost not caring, we let the joyful sensation come, opening our bodies to its gentle influence. Its quality, mild and sweet like milk and honey, touches us deeply, subtly continuing, refreshing itself, increasing until we enjoy an almost overwhelming feeling of fulfillment.

By breathing more subtly, we feel even more; a quality of softness intermixes with the warmth, and our bodies become light and still. Within the body and beyond it, subtle energies nourish feelings of satisfaction and harmony. We become integrated with these feelings, inseparable from them. Our awareness expands, relating many thoughts and feelings simultaneously, and extending their duration. We discover the joy of exercising without effort. We live within a sense of freedom, a vital totality, a feeling which constantly accumulates. Life becomes a constant joyful flow in the vast universe: every cell, every sense, every part of consciousness past or future participates in this flow. In this way, we learn to live cheerfully, even longer, for our lives are healthy and balanced.

As soon as the body and the breath are sufficiently calm and relaxed, immediately, almost magically, the joyful feeling arises. This is the feeling to expand and accumulate, this is the cream of Kum Nye, the essence. We can stir it so that it becomes richer and deeper, more thick and vast. It can become so great it is almost everlasting, and we need never lose it. Its texture is creamy; its very essence, nectar. We can accumulate it and distribute it through the senses, between the skin and muscles, into every part of the body. By this kind of relaxation, we can heal even our grasping, shadow side, the unbalanced side that acts against us. The soothing quality of this feeling can heal thoughts, feelings, concepts, and images, embracing them so there is no longer any negative quality.

When we tap and cultivate the source of relaxation and healing energy within our sensations and feelings, we are doing Kum Nye. *Kum* means body, existence, how to become embodied. Nye means massage or interaction. In Tibetan, *lu* means our ordinary body; *ku* a higher, more subtle body. In Kum Nye, we activate the *ku*, stimulating feeling, which is *nye*.

Whon wc really know how to quicken and develop feelings and subtle energies, cultivating their potential so they continuously feed and nourish themselves in an ever-expanding, flowing way, it is even possible to refine, recreate, and regenerate all of the patterns of the living organism. We can do this because Kum Nye puts us in touch with the pure energies of the body and mind. By increasing our awareness of the immediate feeling-tone of each sensation or emotion, we learn to move within these forms of energy, becoming familiar with different sensory levels until finally we contact the neutral yet totally wholesome energy that pervades all outer forms.

In each Kum Nye exercise, there are three levels at which the exercise may be experienced, corresponding to three different levels of relaxation. At the first level, feelings have a kind of 'tone' such as joy or sadness, warmth or coolness. These feelings are easy to identify and describe: there is perhaps a tingling sensation, a slightly painful sensation, or a feeling of relaxation and energy flowing through the body. These are 'surface' feelings. We feel them in particular locations in the body, and we remain aware of our 'self' experiencing these feelings during the exercise.

By closely attending to these initial feelings or sensations, we can penetrate to a deeper level of feeling. The first layer of feeling opens to a feeling of greater density and toughness, characterized by a holding quality which blocks energy flow. This feeling cannot be exactly identified, but a 'flavor' remains. Although this layer of feeling is more difficult to deepen than the first, it can be gently melted through a kind of open concentration. At this level, there may be a sense of the exercise doing itself, though there is still an awareness of the 'self' feeling the sensation. The self may, however, be experienced as less solid.

At the third level of feeling, we approach pure energy or experience. All residues of patterning are transcended. There is no longer any feeling which can be separated out and identified, only a kind of totally melting quality similar to the open-ended quality of very joyful feelings. This quality does not exist in any particular location. We do not know where or how it is happening, or what it is; it has no quality of 'whatness'. At this level, the individual ego no longer exists, for we become the feeling, totally one with it. This is the stage of fruition, the level of completion which is true relaxation.

Once we tap this relaxation, we learn to operate all sensations and emotions with a playful, open attitude, and everything becomes relaxation. We know that within every feeling or sensation there is the same pure energy—that both 'negative' and 'positive' emotions are flexible manifestations of energy, for only at the surface level do negative and positive, sadness and happiness exist.

Then we know how to use the raw material of experience. At the beginning of any sensation we increase and expand it until it becomes firmly established. When we reach the second layer of feeling we expand that as well, experiencing it fully until we pass into the final stage. When the next feeling or sensation arises, we begin again, creating a continuous circle. Then energy constantly refreshes itself, and all of the patterns of basic existence, the patterns of our living being, are constantly renewed. Time and age cannot catch and freeze this energy, for it is always actively moving, cultivating itself, never delayed or at a standstill. Sometimes we call this process 'longevity', and its potential lies within the senses.

Kum Nye practices are symbols which point us to the nature of all existence. By stimulating the energies of existence, we begin to understand how mind and matter function and interact. We develop an understanding of physical laws—how sensations arise, perceptions develop, concepts come into being, and mental events take place. As soon as we are aware of the energy and potential in all existence, we learn to see, pursue, and experience this potential. We appreciate the vibrant character of physical form, and use this vitality to nourish ourselves. Through feelings, or the energy embodied in physical form, we learn to experience the physical patterns occurring in our bodies, and then understand how matter itself is patterned.

The laws of the universe become transparent to us. We see that our living organism is no different from a cloud taking shape and dissolving away. We no longer see our bodies as fixed, solid things; we experience ourselves as a process of ongoing embodiment which at any particular moment manifests itself as a physical entity and has the capability to continuously regenerate itself. As soon as we see that the body is not a physical machine but an embodiment of values and responsiveness, we begin to understand a way of being which is beyond the usual polarity of 'existence' and 'non-existence'.

When we open to feeling, we no longer see 'energy' only as something that has taken a form with a beginning, middle, and end; we see energy as a complete whole. It has no limitations, no 'outside'; it carries on the character of numberless forms. Yet the word 'numberless' is not accurate, because the energy itself is whole. Therefore, once we understand ourselves, we can understand others; if we understand our own bodies, we can understand universes. The same thing is happening everywhere.

When we expand our awareness far enough, we see energy as having no subject or object relationship at all. There is only one center, and everything becomes the center. Speaking on the ordinary level we could say that the center is both subject and object, but from another dimension there is no subject-object relationship. The center itself has no limitations or forms; it is a complete whole. Everything we look at is the center: universe, body, senses.

Preparation

Even the moment practice begins,
you are planting the seed of a
healthy, positive attitude.

P ractice of Kum Nye is an exploration and balancing of our inner environment. To benefit most from this experience, the external environment should be made as harmonious as possible. The external environment reflects our internal state of mind, and careful preparation can encourage positive internal feelings. As experience of the inner world expands through practice of Kum Nye, as we become more balanced, appreciation of the external world increases effortlessly. With continuing practice, the separation between external and internal gradually melts away, and we naturally interact harmoniously with our environment.

Choose a clean and quiet place, either indoors or outdoors, where you will not be interrupted or distracted. Complete quiet is not always possible in a noisy modern city, so find as quiet a place and time as you can, and encourage those with whom you live to respect your need for time alone. The temperature should be comfortable, neither too hot nor too cold, and the lighting soft. A carpeted floor or a level grassy place make practice especially pleasant. If you are practicing indoors, you may want to open a window to clear the air, or burn incense. Before you begin, take time to become familiar or reacquainted with your surroundings. Perhaps walk as well as look around; investigate any possible distractions until you feel comfortable turning your attention inward.

During practice, wear a leotard or loose, comfortable clothing which gives you maximum freedom of movement. As the senses expand, awareness develops, and sensing the texture and weight of materials becomes part of the pleasure of practice. Remove anything which could obstruct movement or energy flow, including jewelry, watches, glasses, or contact lenses.

For the sitting exercises you will need a cushion so that your pelvis is higher than your legs. If you find sitting on the ground too difficult, then a straight-backed chair is fine. When performing the standing exercises, stand on a carpet or on the floor, not on a thick mat. For the massage, use a lightly-scented massage cream or a vegetable oil such as safflower or olive. If you use vegetable oil, you may want to add a sweet scent, perhaps musk or cinnamon oil.

Creating an environment conducive to practice is an expression of a positive attitude toward yourself—even the moment practice begins, you are planting the seed of a healthy, positive attitude. Intrinsic in practicing these exercises is the decision to find satisfaction within yourself. Nourish this attitude and it will grow within you, developing and increasing your sense of balance, happiness, and relaxation.

All the exercises in this book are ways to touch and expand inner feelings and energies. The external form of the exercise may be stillness, breathing, self-massage, or movement, but the internal exercise or massage, the essence of Kum Nye, is with feeling. From the moment you begin practice, concentrate on the feelings and sensations that arise. Whether you are sitting, standing, or lying down, consider your posture and gestures part of the quality of your experience, and be aware of how they affect your feelings. When you move, do so slowly and rhythmically.

Just as you cannot truly appreciate the scenery from the windows of a speeding train, when you move too fast in a practice, you will not be able to savor the joy of your discoveries. Every movement can be deeply felt and gracefully performed: imagine the feeling a dancer has when beginning to dance. Execute each motion with gentle concentration . . . not a fixated concentration, but a kind of openness that will encourage awareness.

Your experience has an open-ended quality when you learn to practice in this way, for as you perform an exercise, you are aware of the form, texture, and movement of the subtle feelings in your body. Feelings of dullness give way to alert probing and sensing of subtle muscular adjustments and energies; deep insights are then possible.

Participate in each exercise as fully as you can, involving your whole being—your heart, senses, awareness, feelings, and consciousness. Bring all of yourself into the form of the exercise. Let your negative as well as your positive feelings be part of the experience. Then Kum Nye becomes a dance in which you participate totally. You are not 'working with the body', or 'working with the senses', but fully participating and responding.

Become intimate with your feelings without trying to name or label them. When you feel something, keep the energy of the feeling alive as long as possible, letting it expand and fill you. Broaden your feelings; let them be a mandala, expanding in every direction into time and space. You may find deep satisfaction in states that are not only within, but are also beyond the senses. Then everything you do can have the quality of these feelings.

The experience of each exercise or massage has three characteristics: positive, negative, and neutral. These characteristics are not judgments, however, for it is as important to feel and work with negativities as it is to work with positive qualities. Awareness of these qualities is an important part of each exercise. Positive feeling is warm and soft and touches your heart. You may feel negative feeling as a dull, dark sensation in your belly. Neutral feeling is light, balanced, still and calm, part of all space.

Taste your experience as fully as you can, chewing, swallowing, digesting, assimilating, and distributing it to your whole body. You will discover different levels of feeling and experience, and you may become aware of the energy within every molecule and cell. You can then increase your awareness and contact with this energy until finally every part of your body acts as a source of energy. When you realize that energy has no location, no 'here' or 'there' and is abundant and available at any time, then you can truly experience the integration of body and mind.

Approach each exercise openly, without expectation or judgment, for if you begin an exercise with an expectation of a modality, you may cut yourself off from the experience. Judging is one of the obstacles to experiencing. It may sometimes be difficult not to take a critical stance, for we have learned to judge almost constantly. We tend to stand outside ourselves, judging our experience and creating inner dialogue which occupies and freezes our energy: "This feels good," or "I must be doing this wrong."

The key to practicing Kum Nye is not to label, manipulate, or try to make feelings mean something. When a judgment arises in your mind, use it as a signal to go deeper into sensations and feelings. Observe what organs, tissues, and muscles are awakening; go into these places and explore. Do you feel pain, or joy, perhaps warmth or energy? What is the nature of the experience, the tones and qualities?

Although this experience of full participation can be called mindfulness, consciousness, or being aware and sensitive, its nature is unconcerned with naming and defining; there is no longer a critical mind judging. What is happening is what you are doing. You do not need to ask questions or report back to yourself

on what is happening. Your feelings simply express
themselves.

In learning to relax, we tend to think that there is a
goal, and that something must be done to achieve it.
The tendency to make an effort is always in the back
of our minds, and may become an obstacle to relaxation. Notice whether you come to rely on certain prep-
arations. Try not to arrange anything within yourself—just be natural. There is not any specific thing
you must do to relax. When you realize this, you will
learn to relax more quickly.

The way to develop relaxation is not to instruct
yourself. When you become tied up in plans or ex-
planations, you cannot find internal openness. The
secret is just to *be*, without relying on instructions.
This may not be easy. We are used to telling ourselves
that there is a certain way to be or to do things, and
then we attempt to manipulate ourselves into that
mold. When we first relax without instructing ourselves, there is usually the feeling that we 'do not
know how to do it'. As relaxation deepens, however,
this feeling of unfamiliarity passes, and there is only
allowing and continuing.

In these volumes there are many instructions, including how to sit still, how to breathe, and how to do
self-massage and other exercises. These instructions
are important and useful, but when you apply them
skillfully, you do not remain caught up in the external
description. You move beyond the mechanical level
to the level of subtle energy, becoming fully open,
with no holding back.

Holding back is like continually waiting to be relaxed, expecting relaxation to come from somewhere
else. There is a kind of fascinated expectation or
inner dialogue we speculate on our success or fail-
ure, and comment on our 'progress'. In this way it is
possible to spend many hours practicing Kum Nye
without opening to the energies and relaxation within.
So do not let such inner dialogue gain control; relax
and let Kum Nye do itself. Direct your energy so that
it flows freely—physically, mentally, and emotionally.
Be aware and accepting, 'letting go' without seriously
paying attention to your inner dialogue or getting
involved in it. Simply concern yourself with what is
at hand—doing an exercise or massage—and do not
worry about results. Then you can develop the
open-ended attitude.

During practice, do not be concerned with
whether you need more experience or effort to make
the exercises work. Simply open the feeling of relaxation as wide as possible. The more you can do this,
the fewer distractions, problems, thoughts, and con-
flicts will arise. The increasing experience of relaxation will nurture your body; your whole being will
gradually become healthier. You do not have to do
specific exercises to accomplish this change; your
experience of alertness and relaxation is itself the
means to transmute ordinary physical energies. Your
body will act by itself.

When you complete an exercise or a period of massage, sit and immerse yourself in the sensations. This
quiet sitting is also part of the exercise, an opportunity to further develop and expand the feelings which

have been stimulated. Warm, glowing, tingling sensations may surface. Stay with the sensations without trying to hold onto them. No effort is needed. Clinging to the feelings, analyzing or categorizing sensations, will interrupt the flow. Simply remain open, and the energy will stimulate itself.

It will probably take several months before you can truly relax, so it is important to practice regularly. The best way to start is to practice Kum Nye for forty-five minutes twice a day, doing sitting, breathing, and movement exercises in the morning, and self-massage in the evening before going to bed. If you wish to spend less time in practice, set aside forty-five minutes once a day. Wait at least an hour after eating to begin.

Begin slowly and gradually, in a balanced way. There are many exercises presented in these volumes, but it may be wise to limit yourself to three or four for several weeks until there is an inner awakening to the experience of Kum Nye. Take your time with each exercise. Running from one exercise to the next creates a false sense of progress. True progress results less from moving quickly and toward more advanced exercises than from slowly deepening your experience of a single exercise. Spend at least two or three minutes with each repetition of an exercise, developing your ability to work on a particular experience. Each exercise is a universe within itself, and can be fully explored internally.

From time to time, especially in the beginning, you may feel reluctant to practice, as if you are not sure you are willing to relax and feel. Listen to your body to find where you feel reluctant or are holding back, and as you begin Kum Nye, concentrate your energy there. Later when you have had more experience, you will welcome the sensation of new energy in your body.

Your body will naturally seek Kum Nye and, as you practice, it will lead you to the exercises or variations you most need to explore. Sometimes an exercise may happen spontaneously during practice, not because you exert mental or rational control, deciding to do it, but because your feelings naturally take the form of the exercise. Once that happens, you develop greater confidence and respect for your body, and greater understanding of the nature of embodiment. You begin to discover your body of knowledge.

As you explore your body, you will discover sensitive and even painful areas. Breathe into the pain; then exhale slowly and gently, and relax the area. You will find that with the healing effect of the exercises, the pain can be transformed into a deep sweetness.

If a color or image appears during practice, stop and look for a moment. At times you may touch an experience beyond time and space. Energy centers may be opening. As you experience relaxation, the flow of energy within your body may open your heart, dissolving tension there, as well as elsewhere in your body. You will experience an opening of your senses and a heightened sensitivity to taste, color, and sound.

As thoughts slow down, internal harmony arises. A sense of relief and inner sureness comes forth. Eventually you will find that feelings of joy, tranquillity, and harmony expand until you perceive them as expanding out into the universe, and you are aware of nothing else.

Be confident in what you are doing, and do not give up. Encourage yourself, and go patiently through whatever occurs in your practice. Others, even family and friends, may not support you or appreciate what you are doing. But your motive in practice is not merely selfish. We want to do our best for future generations of humanity, for our friends and family, and we must begin by taking care of ourselves.

This may look selfish, but ultimately our knowledge of ourselves will give us more to share with others. In the beginning perhaps we will give seventy-five percent of our time and energy to ourselves, and twenty-five percent to others; later these percentages may be reversed. When we become fully accomplished or enlightened, we can give ourselves completely to others. Then we are free, and everything becomes service.

Sitting

*As thoughts slow down,
internal harmony arises. A sense of
relief and inner sureness
comes forth.*

Kum Nye begins simply, with just sitting still and relaxing. Find a quiet place where you can sit on a mat or cushion, or on a straight chair. The traditional position for sitting (shown by the Buddha when he first became enlightened) facilitates relaxation of both body and mind. Energy flows smoothly in this position, and with enough time, all mental and physical energies become transformed into positive, healing sensation. This position has seven 'gestures'.

The first gesture is to sit with the legs crossed. (For these exercises, however, if it is too difficult for you to sit cross-legged, sit in a straight chair with your legs uncrossed. Sit forward on the seat so you do not lean against the back of the chair, separate your legs a comfortable distance, and place your feet flat on the floor. This allows the weight of the body to be distributed on a firm triangular base.) When you sit cross-legged, arrange your mat or cushion so your pelvis is higher than your legs. Sitting in the half or full lotus (i.e. with one or both ankles resting on top of the thigh) is helpful but not essential.

The remaining six gestures are as follows:

The hands are on the knees, palms down. Release tension in your arms and shoulders, and relax your hands so they rest comfortably on your knees.

The spine is balanced without being rigid. This allows energy to flow naturally from the lower to the upper body.

The neck is drawn back a tiny bit. Your head will move forward very slightly.

The eyes are half-open and loosely focused on the ground, following a line downward along the ridge of the nose. Let your eyes be very soft and compassionate, 'Bodhisattva eyes', like a mother looking at her child.

The mouth is slightly open, with the jaw relaxed.

The tip of the tongue is lightly touching the palate ridge, just back of the teeth. The tongue will curve back a little.

As you sit in this way, try to minimize blinking by relaxing the area around your eyes and moving your awareness inward.

If you are unused to sitting cross-legged, you may feel some discomfort at first, until you learn to relax unnecessary tension. If you have pain in your knees, cross your legs very loosely, and put a higher pillow under your pelvis. The difficulty may be in the knees, but most likely your thigh joints are stiff. The following two exercises will help to loosen the thigh joints. These exercises will also help you if you can sit cross-legged comfortably, but have trouble sitting in the half-lotus or lotus position.

Exercise 1   Letting Go

Sit on a mat or cushion with the soles of your feet together and your hands on your knees. Bring your feet close to your body. With your hands pushing your knees, begin a light, quick, up-and-down movement in your legs, like the flutter of the wings of a bird. Pay attention to the upward movement. Continue for about a minute. Then sit quietly for a few minutes, sensing your body. Repeat three times.

Exercise 2 Melting Tension

Sit on a mat or cushion and cross your legs so your right ankle rests on your left thigh. With your back straight, interlace your fingers and clasp your hands around your right knee. Very slowly lift your right knee a short distance and then lower it. Do this three or nine times, very slowly, feeling the sensations in your body. Then reverse the position of your legs and repeat the movement, three or nine times. When you finish, sit in the sitting posture for five minutes, allowing your sensations to continue.

If you need to change position while sitting, straighten one leg in front of you, and lift the other knee, placing the sole of the foot on the floor. Clasp the knee of the bent leg with both hands, and sit in this position. After a while, reverse the position of your legs. When you feel ready, sit cross-legged again. It is also possible to sit for about ten minutes, massage your legs and feet for a few minutes, and sit again for ten minutes, continuing like that for as long as you wish to sit.

Physical discomfort has a mental or emotional component; when our minds are not at ease, our bodies cannot be relaxed. When you feel uncomfortable while sitting, notice your state of mind. Is there an active flow of thoughts, dialogues, images, and fantasies? In time, you will discover that the sitting posture itself (i.e. the seven gestures) and the soft, smooth breathing it facilitates can relieve both mental and emotional agitation, and physical tension.

In the beginning, you may understand relaxation in a mechanical way, thinking that sitting still means the body does not move; you may hold yourself still. But it is possible to learn to be still without becoming rigid. As you continue to practice, you will discover you do not need to make an effort to relax. Eventually you will experience complete alertness and stillness.

Now sit comfortably in the sitting posture, either cross-legged or on a straight chair, allow yourself thirty minutes to an hour, and try the next two simple exercises.

Exercise 3   Tasting Relaxation

Breathe deeply about ten times, and slowly relax your whole body. Relax your eyes, closing them if you wish, and let your mouth fall open. Let tension slip away from your forehead and scalp. Slowly sense every part of your head—your nose, your ears, your jaw, the inside of your mouth, your cheeks —until your whole head becomes completely relaxed. Then relax the back and sides of your neck, your throat, and the underside of your chin. When you find a tense place, enjoy the sensation of tension melting away. Move to your shoulders, your chest, your arms and hands, your belly, your back, your legs and feet, even your toes. Taste the feeling of relaxation, really feel it, enjoying it more and more until it nurtures every part of your body. Continue for fifteen to thirty minutes.

Exercise 4   Following Sensation

Sit as relaxed and still as you can. Slowly let yourself become aware of any sensation or feeling-tone that arises. At the beginning you may have to remind yourself: remember! Follow whatever happens. You may feel a physical sensation or an emotion. The sensation does not need to be strong . . . it may be light, even delicate. Be attuned to your inner ear. Trust the presence of your experience, and open yourself to it. Do this in whatever way you do it, without method or formulation. Whenever you feel a sensation or feeling-tone, allow it to continue as long as possible. Continue for fifteen to thirty minutes.

For the next week, let yourself be as relaxed as possible during every moment of the day. Relax while eating, shopping, or working. Sensitively watch your movements (even the blinking of your eyes) for subtle patterns of muscle tension. Relax every part of your body as much as you can, including your breath, your skin, and all your internal organs. Even your hair can be relaxed. Let all aspects of your body have a relaxed, gentle quality. Then you can bring your feelings and sensations alive, and they can inspire and nurture you.

Stimulating feelings and expanding them is the basic activity of Kum Nye. In this way, we learn to increase our enjoyment and appreciation of every aspect of living. Even a minute sensation can be increased, accumulated, and expanded until it flows throughout our bodies, and expands even beyond us to the surrounding world.

Exercise 5   Expanding Feeling

Sit down very quietly in the sitting posture, and breathe gently and evenly, with your mouth slightly open. Think about some wonderful memory, and let it become very real. Perhaps you remember one of the most enjoyable times in your childhood, your first love, or a beautiful natural place with fields and a river, where you used to go walking. How do you feel? Create the positive energy of this memory, expanding it more and more. Let your body heat up and your breath move a little higher in your chest, until you feel exhilarated. Close your eyes, and increase the feeling of exhilaration until you really feel it bodily.

Expand the sensation with the whole of your body, so it becomes interpenetrating, and you are not sure if it is inside or outside or where its boundaries lie. Keep expanding the feeling even more, two or three inches outside your body. You are the center of the feeling, and from the center it moves out everywhere, in infinite ripples and layers.

Now slowly draw this vital feeling back into your body; you may almost see it physically. Let this energy unite and cleanse your body and mind.

Continue to exercise your exhilarating feeling in this way for fifteen to twenty minutes, first expanding it, creating more and more of the feeling; then bringing it back into your body and senses. If you do this whenever you have beautiful ideas, images, or feelings, your sensory awareness becomes developed in a finer, more substantial way.

Practice this exercise frequently for the next few weeks, daily if possible.

Breathing

*Once we know how to contact
the energy of breath, breathing becomes an
infinite source of vitalizing energies.*

B ecause breathing charts the life rhythms, the way
we breathe signals the disposition of our energies. Agitation or excitement causes the breath to
be uneven and rapid; but when we are calm and
balanced, our breathing is even, slow, and soft. We
can also change our mental and physical states by the
way we breathe. Even when very upset, we can calm
and balance ourselves by breathing slowly and
evenly.

When breathing is consistently calm and even,
energy increases, and health improves. We can sleep
better. The whole mental and physical organism becomes balanced. The mind becomes lucid, and the
body grows alert and sensitive: hearing is clearer,
colors are more vibrant, and it is possible to savor
more of the flavors of experience. Feeling tones become richer, so certain small things can be enjoyed
tremendously, like a little laughter. Once we know
how to contact the energy of breath, breathing becomes an infinite source of vitalizing energies.

This gentle breathing links us to a flowing sort of energy or 'breath' which is itself inseparable from the subtle mental and physical energies which move throughout the body. This whole 'energy pattern' can be seen as a mandala, an originating center or zero point from which energy flows in all directions. Within this pattern are energy 'centers' which act as 'terminals' for these energies as they radiate and circulate throughout the body. Among these centers are the head center, the throat center, and the heart center. If we could see this energy pattern from a distance, it would look like a spiral with the head center at the top; seen from above, it would appear to be a series of concentric circles with one ring for each of the energy centers.

The energy of 'breath' is particularly associated with the throat center, which both evokes energy and coordinates the energy flow throughout the body. It is therefore through the throat center that we can most easily learn to contact and balance the energy of 'breath' and other subtle energies.

The throat center is traditionally pictured as a sixteen-petaled flower with two blossoms connected back to back. One eight-petaled blossom is directly linked to the head center, the other to the heart center; as energies pass through the throat center, they flow outward to these other centers. When the throat center is settled and calm, the energies flow in a balanced and coordinated way: mental and physical energies become integrated, and 'breath' itself is balanced and purified. Usually, however, the throat center is agitated, so these energies become 'blocked' and do not flow properly.

It is possible, however, to breathe in such a way that the throat center becomes calm and functions smoothly. The way to do this is to breathe slowly and evenly through both nose and mouth, with the mouth slightly open and the tongue lightly touching the palate. In the beginning this is not very comfortable, but as energy begins to travel evenly to the head and heart centers, the vitalizing effects of this way of breathing are felt, and it becomes increasingly easy and pleasant to continue. As the flow of energies within us becomes balanced, our feelings and sensations unfold naturally, and we open to deep sensations of fulfillment.

But this takes time. Because the flow of energies throughout our systems is so often imbalanced, we lose touch with our feelings and sensations. This itself often makes it difficult for us to consistently move toward balance within ourselves. Our old habits of 'reaching out' for satisfaction, of looking for others to give us positive feelings of joy and fulfillment, are hard to break. Yet the more we look outside ourselves for fulfillment, the more we lose touch with ourselves and our inner body sensations. We lose touch with both our physical body and our emotional body.

Once this pattern is in force, it becomes self-perpetuating. Instead of experiencing directly, fully assimilating our sensations and integrating them with the feelings of the heart, we get caught in patterns of thinking *about* our experience, labeling it, and reporting back to ourselves on its nature. We thus reinforce the subject, the 'I' who *does* the experiencing, and experience itself becomes an 'object' frozen into form and meaning.

When we are in this state, our feelings are actually secondary feelings, interpretations of mental images which we then feed back to ourselves. We live 'in our heads', subsisting on records of past experience, mental verbalizations unconnected to our true feelings. A feeling of almost continuous dissatisfaction arises, a subtle form of anxiety which we can feel in the throat center as a kind of tightness, and which manifests as the 'self' reaching out for experience. The flow of energy to the head center increases, and the energy flow to the heart center lessens.

All emotional extremes and imbalances occur in this state: very heightened emotion, like anger or hate, or severe depression and lack of energy. Until the throat center settles, and subtle energies are distributed as much to the heart as to the head, we cannot truly contact our senses or touch our real feelings. Without the energy needed to activate them, our senses are unable to operate properly, and appear to be asleep.

Kum Nye shows us how to gently dissolve this pattern of anxiety and reaching out, and leads us back to direct experience. By breathing softly through both nose and mouth, we can gradually bring the breath to an even level, and balance the throat center so that energies are directed evenly to both the head and heart centers. This steady, even, and yet uncontrolled breathing has a kind of open quality. Even when we first begin to breathe this way, we may feel the senses awaken and begin to stir.

At first, lightly pay attention to breathing equally through both nose and mouth. The quality of the breathing is effortless, without strain. Just let it be natural; you do not need to think about breathing correctly . . . but somehow, way back, your awareness sees that your breath is equally distributed between nose and mouth, and between the inhalation and the exhalation.

As you breathe, your body becomes calm, and you feel relaxed. As soon as you notice the feeling of relaxation, taste and enjoy it. If you do not notice this feeling at first, imagine your ideal of the most heavenly, exquisite feelings. Enjoy them, feel them. Later on you will physically feel the energy. Once you contact the feeling of relaxation, you have found the way. Go into it as deeply as you can; the deeper you go, the richer the feeling becomes, and you can then gather it and bring the harvest to every part of your body. You can feel it even in your bone marrow, and outside your body as well. Wherever you look there is the same feeling.

Then just accumulate the quality of that feeling, stimulating it, making it even richer, deeper, and broader. Encourage the quality of the breath. Let it become exhilarating; accumulate it as water is accumulated to create electrical power. The feeling is joyful, blissful, tremendously open, with a vast merging quality. The feeling can become so vast that there is an almost overwhelming quality, so powerful you feel you cannot take it any more. Finally, when the feeling builds to this power, it can open all your energy centers, cells, and senses; your whole body becomes balanced.

By steadily practicing this breathing and contacting this feeling, you can accumulate it more and more until finally you directly touch its essence. You need no interpretations or words—you will just be there directly. Then any time you want to use that energy you can. Like adding seasoning to food, you will be able to use as much as you like, whenever you need it.

As you develop the quality of your breath, awareness, which arises from direct experience, will gradually expand until breath and awareness become a unity. Then the energies of awareness and breath stimulate each other, and energy increases, always fresh and available. The process is almost like charging a battery: you plug awareness or mental energy into the breath, and stimulate energy. This is the secret of abundant energy. Even if your energy is low at the moment, you have lines to it, and can reach out for it. When you know how to regenerate your energy and keep it in good supply, you can even afford to give it away, for you have an infinite resource.

When breath is truly balanced—not too controlled or tight, but very slow and smooth, at an even level —and when, at the same time, awareness is united with breath as in a marriage, certain effects happen naturally. Breath is then like radar, for you are able to immediately sense the signals of any emotion, your own or others. Your awareness of the beginnings of emotion and feeling is a kind of space which protects you. Awareness becomes an open field which allows you to exercise awakened control, very different from control by suppression or force.

When you are aware of your breath, your whole life becomes balanced. Even when you find yourself in situations which arouse great anger, frustration, or pain, you can dissolve the disturbance by just being aware of your breathing, slightly paying attention and making the breath calm, slow, and rhythmical. The longer you accumulate energy with the breath, the more your whole body calms down; as you give the energy a chance to settle, various parts of the body, at all levels, become quieted. Life has a healthy rhythm, disturbed by few extremes, and the senses can then ripen and mature.

It is important, however, to work continually with the breath, for if you do not, the effects will not last: your body, mind, and senses will slip back into an unbalanced rhythm. So practice this kind of breathing each day for at least three months; twenty to thirty minutes a day is helpful. Try to keep the energy flowing, accumulating and generating it with the breath. First you can be mindful, paying attention to your breathing. Then gradually you will develop a quality of awareness like meditation. It does not matter what you call it—relaxation, awareness, or meditation, for these are all just labels. What is important is the quality of the experience.

Once we learn to accumulate energy, we can carry on this process day and night, not just at certain set times. The whole body becomes relaxed, muscle tension and mental blockages dissolve, and energy is distributed everywhere. Our lives become broader and healthier. Later on we may not even have to make any effort at all to tap this energy of breath, for it is behind all physical and mental energies.

Because both external and internal energies come from the same 'breath' or 'prana', as our inner environment changes, our relationship with the external world changes too, and the universe becomes much more comfortable to be in. It is as if the outer world of objects and our inner world of the senses—our consciousness—were to merge. We support the world, and it supports us and our senses. Our senses give us pleasure, and we feel positive; we project that, and receive back what we project. Inner and outer become harmonized and balanced.

Begin by breathing very easily. As you progress, breathe more slowly. Just let the breath slow down until it eventually becomes totally smooth and even, almost without inhalation or exhalation. Your energy will then steadily increase. As you practice Kum Nye check your breathing from time to time to see how you are progressing toward this goal.

The Exercises

To develop the breathing of Kum Nye—gentle, slow, and even, through both nose and mouth—it is best to practice for twenty to thirty minutes every day for at least three months. In the beginning, it may help to separate out the different qualities of this breathing. For the first week breathe very softly, as in Exercise 6. For the next three or four days, breathe very slowly, as in Exercise 7. If you wish, spend more time on each of these exercises. Then develop an even, balanced breath that is also soft and slow, as in Exercise 8.

In addition, you may want to try some of the other breathing exercises in this section. The sitting position shown in Exercise 10 is a traditional posture for meditation. Try it sometimes after massage or exercising. Exercise 12 is best done in the evening before going to sleep. Exercise 13 is traditionally done on arising in the morning. Exercise 14 is a little more advanced than the other exercises here, and will be most effective if practiced after a few months' experience of Kum Nye.

As you do these exercises, let your breathing nourish and relax you, increasing your feelings of enjoyment until they become so substantial they are almost tangible. Let the breath bring more vitality to your body and greater clarity to your mind. Throughout the day, allow your breathing to sustain and nurture you. Feel how your senses come alive, giving all of your life a magical, spicy flavor.

Exercise 6   Joyful Breath

Sit comfortably in the sitting posture (i.e. the seven gestures), either on a mat or cushion, or on a straight chair. Make sure your mouth is slightly open, with the tip of the tongue lightly touching the palate ridge. Gently relax your throat, belly, and spine. Begin to breathe very softly and easily through both nose and mouth, without paying much attention to the process. This gentle breathing is quite light, yet very energizing. When you feel muscle tension, let the breath touch it gently and loosen it. Bring words and images to the breath and let it soothe and relax them as well. Let this soft breathing quiet and settle your whole body. Without trying to control the breath very much, let it gradually become even more calm and soft until a quality of mellowness develops.

As soon as you feel a sensation—perhaps a feeling of something flowing in your throat and body—accumulate the feeling, not by trying to add anything to it, but by simply allowing it to continue. Feel it more. You may feel the sensation moving to different parts of your body.

Practice this breathing for twenty to thirty minutes a day for about a week. As much as you can, become aware of the quality of your breath throughout the day. After a week, go on to Exercise 7.

Exercise 7   Opening the Senses

Sit comfortably in the sitting posture, and begin to breathe softly through both nose and mouth. Lightly pay attention to the inhalation, and gently slow it down as much as you can, while keeping the breath as soft as possible. Feel the sensations in and around your body as your inhalation slows down, and go deeply into them, expanding and accumulating them with the breath. Continue for ten to fifteen minutes.

Now lightly pay attention to the exhalation, and exhale very slowly through both nose and mouth, keeping the breath light and soft. (As you do this, do not try to do anything special with the inhalation.) As you develop the quality of this slow exhalation, try to open the whole sensory field as much as possible— every cell, tissue, and organ. Let your feelings spread like a halo throughout and around your body. Continue for ten to fifteen minutes.

Practice this slow breathing for twenty to thirty minutes for three or four days. On the third and fourth days, practice twice a day if you can. After you increase the time, pay a little more attention to the quality of your breathing, following your breath with your awareness until you become very still. After the third or fourth day, go on to Exercise 8.

Exercise 8   Living Life in the Breath

Sit comfortably in the sitting posture, and breathe softly and slowly through both nose and mouth. Gently pay attention to breathing so that the breath flows equally through both nose and mouth. Give equal time to inhaling and exhaling.

Notice the quality of your breathing, how sometimes it may be hard and choppy, sometimes agitated or deep. Notice how the different qualities of breathing are related to different mental and feeling states, and how as your breathing becomes easier and more even, your mind settles, and feeling flows.

As you breathe, open the feeling of relaxation as wide as you can. Unite your awareness with your breath, and expand any sensations that arise until you no longer know where the boundaries of your body lie; there is only feeling and the subtle energy that rides on the breath.

As breathing becomes more even, you naturally grow more calm. Superfluous muscle tensions dissolve, releasing different layers of feeling. As you penetrate to deeper layers of feeling, you will become familiar with many subtle feeling-tones, although you may not necessarily have words to describe them. Let these feeling-tones expand so that they become deeper and more vast.

Practice this even breathing for twenty to thirty minutes every day for at least three months. Then continue to practice this breathing whenever you can, when working, walking, talking—during every moment of your daily life, and even during the night, when you awaken.

You may sometimes want to practice this breathing while lying down on your back, either with your legs straight, or with your knees bent and your feet flat on the floor.

In Exercises 9, 10, and 11, a mantric syllable—OM, AH, or HUM—is silently chanted and unified with the breath. In Exercise 12, the mantra OM AH HUM merges with the breath. You do not need to actually pronounce these sounds; simply be aware of them.

OM signifies the energy of existence; AH symbolizes interaction; HUM, creativity. OM signifies physical form. AH represents the energy which informs and keeps alive the physical form. HUM symbolizes thoughts, awareness, and activities. OM AH HUM symbolizes the enlightened body, mind, and spirit.

Exercises 9, 10, and 11 can be practiced for either short periods of time, or for long periods such as four or five hours. You might want to begin practicing one of these exercises for a half hour. When you become familiar with the exercise, try lengthening the time to an hour or more.

Exercise 9   OM

Sit comfortably in the sitting posture. Breathe gently
and evenly through both nose and mouth, and be
aware of the syllable OM. Begin to chant OM inwardly, as if chanting with the breath. Let OM and the
breath become inseparable. Develop the feeling qualities of breathing OM as fully as possible. You may
feel a rising, allowing motion like inhaling, and a
gentle, awakened quality to your awareness.

Exercise 10   Ah

Sit comfortably. Bring your hands in front of your belly, cradle the fingers of the right hand in the fingers of the left hand, and lift the thumbs a little and join them. Breathe gently through both nose and mouth, and silently begin to chant Ah within the breath, letting Ah and the breath become one. You may feel a very silent, concentrated quality, and the breath may become very still.

Exercise 11   HUM

Sit cross-legged on a mat or cushion, and place your
hands on your knees, with the palms up. Breathe
gently through both nose and mouth, and be aware of
HUM. Bring HUM into the breath, unifying sound and
breath. Develop the feeling quality of this sound-
breath as fully as possible. You may feel a subtly
sharp, penetrating awareness, a letting go as if
exhaling, and a fresh, radiant clarity.

Exercise 12   Breathing OM AH HUM

This exercise is best practiced in the evening before going to sleep. Lie down on your back on the floor with your arms at your sides. Separate your legs about the width of your pelvis. Support your head with a pillow if you are more comfortable that way, and also put a pillow under your knees. Open your mouth slightly and lightly touch the tip of your tongue to your palate. Breathe gently and even'y through both nose and mouth. As you breathe, be aware of the mantra OM AH HUM.

During the inhalation, visualize or think about OM. Hold the inhalation slightly and that becomes AH. When you are ready to exhale, think HUM. Do not actually pronounce the mantra; just be aware of OM AH HUM. Breathe smoothly and casually, giving equal time to inhaling and exhaling.

When holding the inhalation, hold in your lower stomach; as you exhale, let the breath go equally from your stomach, nose, and mouth. Breathe a little heavily to start; gradually and without effort, decrease the amount of air you take in until your breathing becomes very slow, and almost silent. At the end of each breath, be very still. After a while your breath will continue as if by itself. Gradually change the focus of your attention from your body to the realm of feeling and energy. It is as if your body expands to a less physical dimension.

Continue for half an hour.

Exercise 13   Cleansing Breath

This breathing is best done immediately on arising in the morning, although it can also be done at other times of the day. It is used traditionally to rid the system of the impurities which accumulate during the night and to renew the body energies in preparation for the new day. While doing the exercise, imagine that you are blowing out from the left nostril all the attitudes with which you push things away from you, including aversion, dissatisfaction, and fear.

Imagine that you are blowing out from the right nostril all the attitudes and emotions with which you hold onto things, including desire, attachment, and anger; and imagine that you are blowing out from both nostrils the dull and confused quality of your everyday mind.

Sit cross-legged on a mat or cushion, and hold your right hand in the position indicated in the drawing, with the thumb held under curled fingers, and the index finger straight. Rest your left hand lightly on your left knee. Inhale very, very deeply, taking in as much air as possible, filling your belly and chest, and even the spaces at the top of the rib cage. Imagine that this breath fills every cell in your body. Then place the middle joint of your right index finger against your right nostril, closing it tightly. Close your mouth, and exhale slowly through your left nostril as deeply as possible, getting the very last bit of air out. Keep exhaling until your stomach begins to quake. Then rest for a moment or two, breathing normally through both nostrils. Repeat twice.

Now do the exercise three times on the right side, closing the left nostril with the middle joint of the left index finger. Rest briefly after each exhalation. Finally exhale from both nostrils three times as fully as possible. When you think you have the last bit of breath out, try to expel more. Then sit for a few minutes, breathing normally and enjoying the sensations in your body.

You can visualize the impurities coming out of your body as a dull white stream from the left nostril, a dark red stream from the right nostril, and a deep blue out of both nostrils.

Exercise 14 Feeling Breath

Sit comfortably in the sitting posture. Inhale through both nose and mouth, and hold the breath for one minute, experiencing and expanding the feeling quality. Let your internal rhythm slow down, and your senses open. You may feel a rippling or vibrating quality like the energy at the edges of a flame. Whatever feelings and sensations arise, deepen and expand them. Experience them directly, without letting them go into concepts or thoughts or mental images. Then exhale slowly. Repeat the exercise three times.

If you find it difficult to hold the breath for one minute, hold it as long as you can. As you continue to practice the exercise, gradually build up to holding the breath for one minute.

Massage

Our feelings and our bodies
are like water flowing into water.
We learn to swim within the
energies of the senses.

The practice of Kum Nye integrates feelings directly with the body, instead of channeling them
through the mind. Our feelings and our bodies are
like water flowing into water. First we 'float' in
feelings of openness, gentle love and joy, relaxing and
letting the feelings themselves buoy us up; later there
is a lifting feeling of complete confidence. As we become used to contacting these feelings and the cur-
rents of energy they produce, we learn to swim
within the energies of the senses. A feeling of unity
and wholeness arises . . . thoughts, senses, mind, and
consciousness join in a kind of inner alchemy. When
Kum Nye massage is done daily for at least six weeks,
these feelings become more and more tangible, occurring not only during practice, but throughout the day.
    This internal 'swimming' or massage melts ac-
cumulated tension, gently releasing the energy which
has been frozen at a subtle level by our fixed attitudes
and concepts. This released energy flows into feeling
experience which then fills every cell in the body.
Our bodies become less solid, more fluid and open,

more *ku* than *lu*. As we live and work closer to the
energy of feeling and experience, thoughts and feelings merge into one; our feelings no longer need to
be accompanied by mental commentary. We find
that direct experience is far more substantial and
grounded than that channeled through thoughts and
imaginings. We grow in awareness.

The immediacy of our experience is lost when we
allow our minds to grasp at our feelings. So when you
begin Kum Nye massage, let go of any preconceptions
or associations you may have. Thoughts and concepts move on a surface layer; as much as you can, go
by degrees to a deeper level, the level of experience.
Explore each feeling fully. Encourage feelings of joy.
Imagine you are in paradise; bring in positive memories, perhaps of beautiful fields, trees, streams,
or mountains. Let the feelings express themselves.
Happiness is a feeling within your organism which
you can stimulate and develop by giving each feeling
more flavor, and feeling it as much as you can. Expand each feeling through your senses and thoughts.
Thoughts then cannot catch you, for you are beyond
ego and self-image.

When you continue to deepen and expand a
feeling, you will find different feeling-tones which
can be explored further. Once you move inside a
feeling, it will expand itself in an inner massage. At
first a feeling will bring to mind various images. At a
deeper level, the feeling will be deeply nurturing,
without images. Finally, you become the feeling, and
there is no longer any experiencer or I. Then you are
deepening, openness, satisfaction, and completion.

Massage means interaction. When you massage yourself, you are not affecting only one place on your body; your whole body participates in the massage. A reciprocal relationship develops between your hand and the muscle or point massaged, generating feelings which stimulate interactions throughout the body. Interaction also occurs between physical and nonphysical levels of existence, and this interaction stimulates certain energies which, not restricted to the body's boundaries, spread to the surrounding world.

When you develop self-massage, you will discover many different kinds of sensations and feelings. Kum Nye massage is oriented toward pressure points which stimulate specific energies. You may find that pressure on some places has an immediate effect; pressure on other places may not affect you noticeably in the beginning. Touching particular spots may restore memories or past negativities. As you rub and release pains and knots in your physical body, you may also release mental and emotional blockages.

Muscular patterns related to old injuries may melt down into pure feeling or experience. Pressing certain points may release loving, joyful feelings which open your heart, merging body and mind into one. As your body becomes more fluid and open, you may even discover a time when there is no special purpose to your massage—it is not oriented toward ego or self. Without preparation or goal it just spontaneously happens, is instantly there.

Once the shape of your tension melts down, only feeling or experience is left. Do not label or identify the nature of the feeling, but simply allow it to continue to melt until it flows completely into itself, filling each center, cell, and sense organ with pure energy and experience, like water flowing to the deepest root of a beautiful rose.

As you massage yourself, stretch the bonds of your ordinary conceptions. When you press a certain point on your body, no part of your body, and in fact no part of the universe, need be excluded. Everything can become part of the massage. From a cosmological point of view, everything participates in the cosmos, and we and the universe are integrated. Our body is like a vessel filled and surrounded by space. When we touch our substance, we stimulate ourselves and the universe simultaneously. Our whole body exercises in space.

The Massage

The best way to begin is to massage yourself for forty-five minutes or more every evening for at least six weeks. After six weeks you may want to continue with the evening massage, or perhaps you will want massage to be a part of your daily Kum Nye practice. Although it is best done in the evening, massage can also be done at other times.

During the massage, wear no clothes, or loose-fitting clothes you can easily open, and remove jewelry, glasses, contact lenses, etc. Perhaps take a hot shower or bath beforehand; this will help relax tense muscles, and open the body to feeling. Use a massage cream or a vegetable oil such as safflower or olive, perhaps with a sweet scent added. After the massage, apply a natural perfume or, if you wish, burn incense. If you are doing the massage right before going to bed, drinking a cup of hot milk with two teaspoons of honey will often help you sleep.

To begin the massage, energize your hands in the way described on page 61. Then slowly oil and rub your body in a random way, without trying to do anything special. Follow your feelings, letting them guide you to where you need especially to rub, and letting them tell you when to increase or decrease pressure. In areas where you feel pain, rub and press with special sensitivity and thoroughness. Let the feelings and the massage move together in rhythm, like music. In this way, slowly massage every part of your body—wherever you can reach. Do not neglect your arms, legs, or feet.

Gradually deepen the experience of the massage, unifying breath, body, senses, and mind. Breathe very slowly and lightly through both nose and mouth; then the breath can awaken and merge with sensation, developing a vital penetrative quality which spreads throughout the body, releasing congested or entangled energies into pure feeling and energy. Expand feeling and sensation to encompass thoughts, so that as you rub and press, your hand becomes the eye of your mind, and your mind enters your body. At the end of the massage, sit still for five or ten minutes and feel the subtle ripples of sensation spreading outward from your body.

After two or three evenings of this sort of 'random' massage, begin to incorporate some of the specific instructions for massage in the pages that follow. Do not rush to try everything, but explore a few new techniques at a time. In the beginning, emphasize your face, head, neck, shoulders, and chest. But always feel free to experiment. Find points of stress and blockage and loosen them, slowly freeing the body from its tight inner and outer harness.

Each time you begin Kum Nye massage, awaken the sensitive energies of your hands. Remember that your hand is not a mechanical tool; it is capable of touching your whole body when it appears to touch only a part. Develop the feelings in the palm, and in each finger and thumb. Whenever possible, use your whole hand to massage; develop reciprocity between your hand and the part you are massaging, and be aware of subtle linkages to other parts of the body.

Energizing the Hands

This massage will animate your hands. Do it whenever you begin massage.

Sit comfortably with your back straight, breathe gently through both nose and mouth, and relax. Oil your hands lightly. Bend your arms at the elbows and hold your hands open, with the palms up, at the level of your heart. Cup your hands a little as if holding energy in them. Feel the sensations—perhaps tingling or warmth—in your hands and fingers. Hold the energy in your fingers; then let it pass into your hands like a flame reaching and spreading. From your hands let the energy pass into your arms, and through your arms into your heart. Allow your whole body to feel deeply nourished by these sensations of energy.

Once you feel these sensations, slowly bring your hands together and rapidly rub the back of your left hand with the palm of your right. You can do this movement quite hard and fast. Follow the sensations—you may feel energy going into your heart and neck and the middle of your back. Reverse the position of your hands, and rub briefly. Now rub your palms together in a rapid motion until they definitely feel hot.

Once again hold your hands open, palms up, at the level of your heart, cupping them a little. Take another minute to feel the sensations flowing in your hands and body, and then slowly begin the massage.

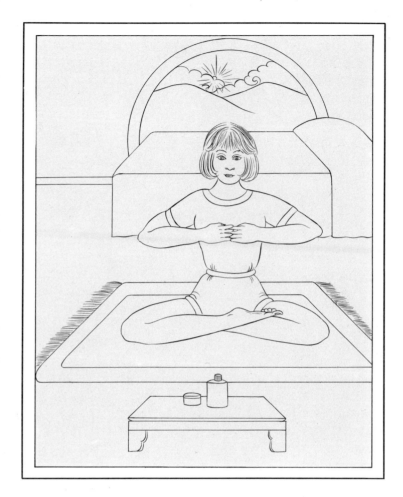

Hand Massage

Massaging your hands can tune, tone up, and enliven the energy of your whole body.

☆ Interlace your fingers tightly with the palms and fingers toward you. Pull under tension, massaging down the fingers until they spring apart in release. Repeat, feeling the sensations awakened in your body.

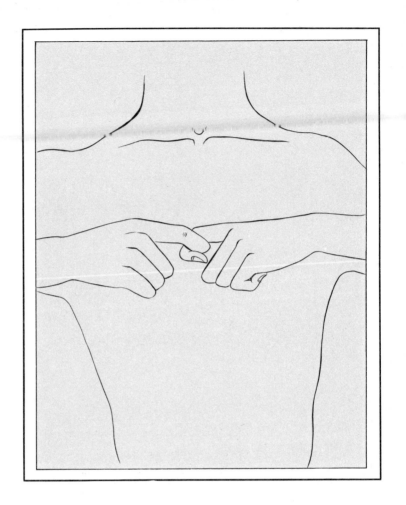

☆ Hook each finger separately with the corresponding finger of the opposite hand. Pull under tension
until the two fingers gradually slip apart.

☆ Massage each fingertip on one hand with the fingertips of the other hand.

☆ Massage down each finger from the fingertip to
the base. Move slowly, making sure to work the sides
as well as the front and back of each finger.

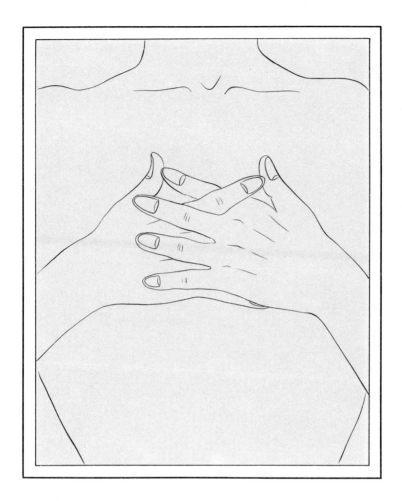

☆ Place the base of the finger to be massaged in the 'web' between the index and middle finger of the other hand, and grasp the finger firmly. Slowly pull the finger while twisting it gently, moving from the base of the finger to its tip.

☆ Work on the back of your hand between each of the small bones, the metacarpals, massaging in the direction of your fingers. Give particular attention to the large area between the forefinger and the thumb.

☆ Massage the palm of your hand with the thumb of the other hand. You can also use the larger knuckle of the forefinger to move across the palm. Deeply massage the large mound of the thumb as well as the smaller mounds below the fingers. Massage between each finger. Pay attention to all of the small muscles between the bones, tracing them from the heel of the hand to the fingers. As you massage, breathe softly and evenly through both nose and mouth.

The next part of the hand massage uses pressure points. As you press these points (and later when you press points on other parts of your body), be very aware of the effects which are produced by different degrees of pressure. At first press very lightly; gradually develop medium pressure; when appropriate, press strongly. When you want to diminish the pressure, do so very gradually: first subtly lighten the strong pressure, then reduce it to medium, and then slowly to light pressure. In this way you can develop awareness of six distinct stages of the massage. With more practice, you may develop additional subtleties of pressure.

Be careful not to release pressure suddenly. This 'shocks' the system and loses the subtle qualities of the feeling. Experience fully the lifting up and putting down of your hand and fingers. When you remove your hand from your body at the end of the massage, do so almost imperceptibly; then the feelings will continue for quite a long time.

☆ The hands have many sensitive and powerful points which stimulate interactions throughout the body. To find the first point, turn your hand palm up and look at the 'rings' at the inside of the wrist. Place your forefinger in the middle of the ring nearest your palm. Then turn your palm down and place your thumb on the second point, which is on the back of your hand exactly opposite the first point. Hold your wrist tightly between your thumb and forefinger, and press strongly. Relax your chest and belly and any other places where you have unnecessary tension; breathe gently through nose and mouth.

Now reverse the position of your thumb and forefinger, placing your forefinger on the back of your hand
and the thumb on the inside of the wrist. Strongly
press and manipulate the two points simultaneously.
Release the pressure gradually, sensing the feelings
that arise.

Keeping your thumb on the same point on the
inside of the wrist, move your forefinger about a
finger-width down towards the fingers and to the side
nearest your little finger. This point (point 3 in Figure
1), between the bones of the little finger and the
fourth finger, may be very sensitive. Once you have
found this place, exert strong pressure with both
thumb and forefinger and hold. Release slowly and
gently.

Now move your forefinger to the corresponding
point on the side of your hand nearest the thumb
(point 4 in Figure 1). This point is approximately one
finger-width down and to the side of the second
point. Again press strongly with both thumb and forefinger and hold. You may feel strong sensations, even
pain. Stay with the feelings, breathing gently through
nose and mouth. Release the pressure gradually.

Now turn your hand palm up. Measure two
finger-widths down (toward the fingers) from the first
point to the fifth point, and place your thumb there.
Then place your forefinger on the point on the back of
your hand exactly opposite this point (i.e., point 6).
Strongly press these two points simultaneously. Release slowly, breathing evenly through both nose and
mouth.

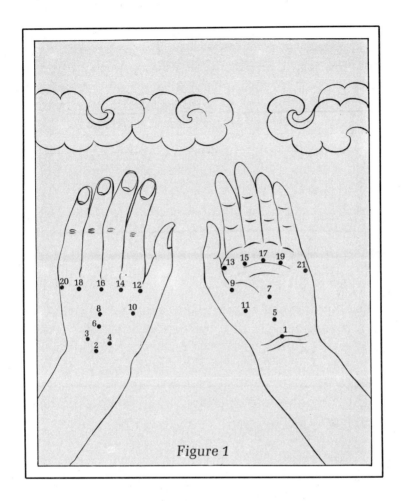

Figure 1

Place your thumb on the point in the middle of your palm (point 7). Place your forefinger on the corresponding point on the back of the hand, between the bones of the middle and fourth fingers (point 8). Press these two points simultaneously in a sensitive way, gradually increasing the pressure. Release slowly.

Now place your thumb on the point near the thumb webbing (point 9). Place your forefinger on the opposing point on the back of the hand (point 10). Press these two points simultaneously, sensitively increasing and decreasing the pressure. Remember to breathe gently through both nose and mouth.

Now place your thumb on the point in the middle of the thumb mound and press and rub sensitively (point 11). The pressure can be strong.

The remaining ten hand points (points 12–21) are in a row across the knuckles. There are five on the palm, and five on the back of the hand. Two pairs of points are at the sides of the hand, and three pairs are between the knuckle-bones. Work these points in pairs, placing your thumb on each palm point and your forefinger on the corresponding point on the back of the hand. Slowly increase and decrease the pressure.

Do the complete massage, including the pressure points, on both hands.

Face Massage

Our heads are usually busier than the rest of our bodies, and emotions—which are closely connected to thoughts—tend to constrict our facial muscles as well as our necks and shoulders. As you massage your face, feel the energy move throughout your body.

☆ Energize your hands in the way described on page 61. Once your palms feel hot, slowly bring them up to your face and place them gently over your closed eyes, without any pressure on the eyeballs, and without touching your nose. Your fingers will overlap a little. Leave your hands in this position for several minutes, sensing the movement of heat and energy into your eyes. Notice connections with other parts of your body; you may feel heat penetrate through the eyeball into many parts of your body.

Again rub your palms together. When they feel hot, place one hand on your forehead and the other on your chin. Close your eyes and feel the energy flow. Repeat, reversing the position of your hands.

☆ Massage around the orbit of your eyes, touching each point firmly and gently. Massage both eyes at the same time. Begin at the inner upper edge of the eye socket, and use your thumbs to find a notch in the bone just under the eyebrow (points 1 in Figure 2). Press up, gradually increasing the pressure, and hold. Keep your head erect. Close your eyes and go into the feelings; they may be quite powerful. Release the pressure very gradually, and stay with the feelings which are produced.

With your first or middle finger, trace under the upper ridge a very short distance from the first point to the next small valley or notch (points 2 in Figure 2), and press and massage it gently. You may want to close your eyes as you do this.

Trace under the upper ridge to the third small valley or notch, near the arch of the eyebrow. Spend extra time here, pressing and massaging gently with

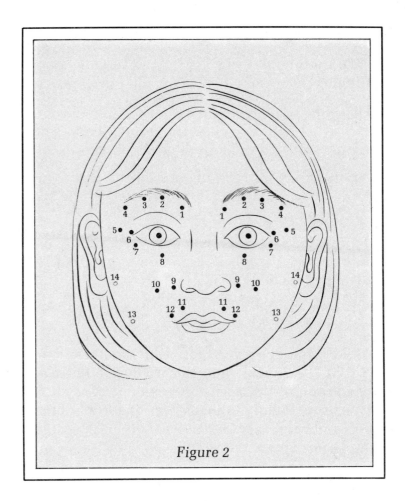

Figure 2

your first or middle finger. Experiment with different degrees of pressure.

At the upper outside corner of the eyesocket there is another place that deserves special attention (points 4). Use the tip of your first or middle finger to locate and massage this small crater in the bone.

Follow the curve of the eyesocket down to a little bump in the bone, a finger-width from the corner of the eye (points 5). Press with your forefingers, gradually increasing and decreasing the pressure.

Use your forefinger to move just inside the corner of the eyesocket to the sixth point. Press gently, breathing softly through both nose and mouth.

Trace with your forefingers a short distance to the seventh point, just inside the eyesocket, a little below the sixth point. Press gently.

Follow the lower curve of the eyesocket to a notch in the bone below the center of the eye (points 8). Press gently and delicately.

Give particular care to the area where the lower eyesocket meets the bone of the nose.

☆ Hold your eyebrows between thumb and forefinger, at the inner edge. Press your thumbs up a little so they rest against the bone and give support from below. Lightly squeeze the eyebrow between thumb and forefinger, and rub slowly back and forth with the forefinger. Work out to the outer edge of the eyebrow; then return to the inner edge and repeat the massage.

☆ With your middle fingers, press and rub the deep depression in the temples. Rub very slowly in a circular motion. When you find a sensitive spot, move even more slowly. Press very lightly at first, and gradually increase the pressure. Be sure to release the pressure very slowly. Then change the direction of the circles, and continue to massage, letting your feelings guide your rhythm and pressure.

☆ To massage your forehead, place the fingers of both hands side by side on the left side of the forehead. Slowly draw your hands horizontally across your forehead, bringing as much of your hand in contact with your forehead as you can. Move slowly back and forth several times.

☆ Now massage down the sides of your nose. Begin with your forefingers on each side of your nose near the corners of your eyes, and rub slowly and thoroughly with an up-and-down motion. You can also use two fingers or even all your fingers, although the forefingers are enough for the job. Move slowly down the sides of your nose, varying the pressure. Give special attention to the areas:

where the bone of your nose ends, about halfway down your nose;

where your nose flanges meet your cheek; and

below your nose, where your teeth begin (see points 11 in Figure 2).

At these places press your fingers in deeper and then rub slowly back and forth. Pay attention to any special feelings that may be released. When you finish rubbing at the base of your teeth, begin to move upward again. Do this complete movement two or three times.

☆ Place your thumbs at the corner where your nose flanges meet your cheek. Your hands will hang down in front of your chin. While pressing your thumbs into this corner, slowly rotate your hands until your fingers point toward the ceiling. Pressing strongly up under the cheekbones, very slowly rub your thumbs back and forth across the area just below the cheekbones, out to the side of your face. The movement of your thumbs is quite subtle although the pressure is strong. Follow the line of the cheekbone up to the bony ridge near the ear. Let your sensations expand, releasing subtle tensions under the skin.

☆ With your forefingers, press points 9, which are on
either side of the nose (see Figure 2). As you gradually
increase the pressure, breathe evenly through both
nose and mouth, and allow your sensations to expand. Do not hesitate to develop strong pressure.

Then follow the line of the cheekbone away from
the nose to points 10, just past the curve. Again, press
strongly, gradually increasing and decreasing the
pressure.

☆ Slowly massage across your cheek to the point just on the corner of the jawbone (points 13 in Figure 2). Press gently here with your forefingers, yawn a little, and slowly move your elbows out to the sides, so your chest feels as if it is opening. Do not press heavily on this point. Continue to press, yawn, and open your chest a little more. Relax your belly, and keep your breath slow and gentle. Then slowly let your elbows come forward, and release the pressure.

☆ Now place your fingers under your jaw and rest your thumbs on your chin, as shown in the drawing. Your elbows will point out to the sides. Using all the fingers at once, press up under the jawbone and work very thoroughly along the whole line of the jaw. Do not be afraid to press strongly. Remember to release the pressure slowly. You will also be able to press along the top of the jawbone with your thumbs. Breathe gently through nose and mouth as you press.

☆ Place your thumbs under your jaws, near the throat, resting your fingers on your chin. Open your mouth slightly, and gently press your thumbs up under the jaw. Manipulate this whole area with your thumbs, slowly pushing up, especially near the root of the tongue and the tonsils. This area may feel thick and gunky; notice if you feel reluctant to touch it. Create a dialogue between your thumbs and these neglected muscles and see if you can bring this area alive. Relax into whatever feelings come up as you press. The musculature of the jaw often holds tight habit patterns of thought and behavior, and massage here may release many different feelings.

With your hands in the same position as above, use your fingers to massage along the upper line of the jaw.

☆ Smile, and manipulate the corners of your smile with your thumbs. You will discover habitual muscle tightenings which you can relieve with this massage. As you rub, you may also be able to massage the gum and the base of some upper teeth through the skin. When you finish rubbing, very slowly relieve the pressure. How does your face feel?

☆ At this point in the massage, when you have covered all of the major areas of the face, it is especially pleasurable to massage the whole face in a slightly different way.

Massage up the center of your forehead and across the forehead to the temple area.

Then massage from the bridge of your nose across the cheeks toward the ear.

Massage across your face from the area under the nose to the ear.

Massage around your mouth, feeling the bone structure underneath your skin. Press points 11 and 12 as shown in Figure 2 with your forefingers.

Massage across your face from the mouth, deeply manipulating the chewing muscles.

Massage along the edge of the chin to the angle of the jaw.

☆ Place one hand across your forehead and the other hand directly above it on your head, with the fingers of each hand pointing in opposite directions. Simultaneously move both hands slowly in the directions the fingers point; then slowly move them back. Continue rubbing back and forth in this way, slowly moving your hands down your face to your chin, then back up again to your forehead. Let your hands contact your face as much as possible. Try this massage after taking a shower.

☆ This massage is for both face and head. Place one hand across your forehead and the other hand across the back of your head. (Be sure to remove glasses and jewelry.) Slowly move your hands in opposite directions, one hand across your face, the other across the back of your head; then move them back. You may feel as though your hands are rotating your head, although your head is motionless during the massage. Continue, slowly lowering your hands until you massage your whole head. Continue past your chin to the throat and the back of the neck. Enjoy the full contact between hand and head.

☆ Use your thumbs and forefingers to massage your ears. Start at the outer edge of the ear and gradually work toward the center in a spiral movement. Manipulate and massage each tiny section, breathing softly and evenly through both nose and mouth, merging breath and feeling. If your ears become hot, gently stop.

☆ Just behind the earlobe there is a small crevice. Close your eyes, and with your forefingers, press and rub near the top of the crevice, very carefully and sensitively, without much pressure. (These are points 14 in Figure 2.) You may feel a connection with your nostrils. Close your mouth and continue to rub very slowly and not too strongly while inhaling through the nose only. Bring whatever sensations you feel into the massage. As you continue to press and rub, inhale a little more through the nose, flaring your nostrils, and relaxing your lower body. Keep your back straight. Then rub more and more slowly, feeling the sensations in your body, until finally you stop rubbing.

Now place your thumbs on this point, press lightly, and with your forefingers slowly rub your temples in circles, first in one direction, and then in the other. Breathe softly and evenly through both nose and mouth, and as you rub, let the breath accumulate sensation and distribute it to every cell of your face, head, and body.

☆ Massage your face with special attention to what is bone and to what is not.

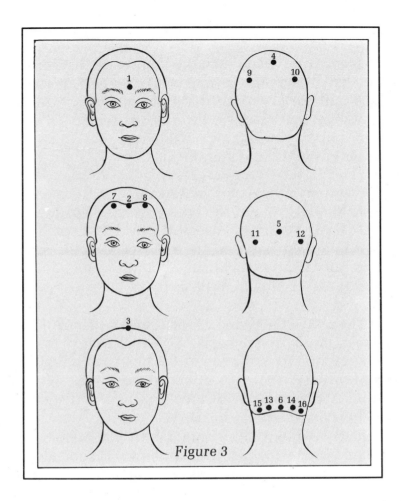

Figure 3

Head Massage

Usually we are more aware of our faces than of the rest of our heads. But the head has sensitive areas and points which can relieve subtle blockages throughout the body, gently awakening the senses.

☆ Massage your scalp with all your fingertips. Separate your fingers and place the fingertips firmly on the front of the scalp with the thumbs on the sides of the skull. Keeping the fingertips in place, massage back and forth so that the scalp moves across the skull. Try this massage at different tempos. Touch every part of your scalp, moving from the front to the center of the back of your head.

☆ Starting at the top of your head, trace the muscles down the left side of the back of your scalp to your neck, using all of the fingers of your left hand. Then use your right hand on the right side of the scalp. Keep your head straight as you do this. Spend extra time at places of pain or pleasure.

☆ The rest of the head massage deals with a group of sixteen pressure points (see Figure 3). Points 1–6 are on a midline over the top of the head, running from front to back. Points 7–16 are found to the sides of points 2, 4, 5, and 6. With a few exceptions, the points are four finger-widths apart.

Gently explore these points until you become familiar with the feelings they stimulate. Do not neglect the side-points. As you rub and press them, breathe slowly and evenly through both nose and mouth, unifying breath and sensation. Go deeply into the feelings stimulated at each point, paying particular attention to the variations in sensation that are produced by different degrees of pressure. Especially as you slowly release the pressure, sense the subtle flavors of feelings that develop.

Once you are familiar with the points, you may want to develop the longer massages such as those for points 3 and 6.

POINT 1:   To find this point, commonly called the 'third eye', measure four finger-widths up from the tip of your nose. To do this, place the fingers of your right hand on the nose so that the little finger rests on the tip and the forefinger is near the eyebrows. Keep your fingers close together and straight. The point is just beyond the forefinger. When you put pressure on this point you may feel a slight depression and a special sensitivity which indicates the right spot.

Place your middle finger on this point, and rub straight up about an inch and then down again, exerting some pressure. Close your eyes and look inside in a relaxed way, concentrating on the point. With eyes closed you feel more as you rub, and the feelings are more likely to continue when you cease rubbing. Breathe gently through nose and mouth. When you sense a kind of energy, transmit layers of this feeling to the center of your body. Once you feel the energy there, slowly distribute the feeling from the center outward to your whole body, letting it become part of every muscle. After about two minutes, let the rubbing subside gently, and sit quietly with your hands on your knees, continuing to sense the feelings which have been produced.

Tension is closely related to the process by which our minds produce images. Rubbing this place relieves much of that tension and stimulates the senses so feelings begin to spread throughout the body like an inner halo. Body awareness and mental awareness merge, united with the breath.

As this relaxation deepens, the ideas and images we produce become more balanced and vital, and of more benefit to others. Our bodies and minds are richly nourished and sustained from within, and we are able to be truly caring to everyone. We are able to use each moment's precious opportunity to expand and share the joy of being alive: as our joyful feeling spreads to others, they also become more balanced.

Pressing the next group of points will help to release muscle tension throughout your body.

POINTS 2, 7, and 8:   Measure four finger-widths from point 1 to point 2. With the first and middle fingers of one hand, press this point, and without lifting up, massage one inch above the point and then down again. Repeat several times.

Massage points 7 and 8, which are an inch to each side of point 2, using both forefingers. Then again massage point 2. Alternate pressure on point 2 and points 7 and 8 for several minutes.

POINT 3:   Measure four finger-widths from point 2 to point 3. This special place is the healing center of the body; it is also the gate through which consciousness passes when we die. Through massage and visualization, we can gently open this center and learn to heal ourselves.

☆ With three fingers, draw a circle at this point, rubbing and pressing lightly. As you rub, visualize a circle two inches in diameter. Close your eyes and slowly lift up your fingers, touching your hair softly. Very slowly raise your fingers higher, two or three inches above this point, and then slowly lower them. Continue to lift and lower your fingers slowly until you feel something, perhaps an open or cool feeling.

Do not be concerned if you do not feel anything special at first. It may take a while. Just continue to concentrate loosely on this point while sensing with your fingers. Later it may be possible to feel a little energy there when rubbing with only one fingertip.

☆ Once you are able to visualize a circular opening on the top of your head, visualize the extension of this circle into an open column from the top of your head to the base of your torso. Spend four or five one-hour sessions if you want to develop this visualization.

☆ When you are able to clearly visualize the open column within your body, visualize sparkling white universal energy pouring into it. This beautiful white energy slowly fills the column, flowing down into your throat, heart, and navel areas, reaching to the very root of your body. The energy is inexhaustible; you can hardly imagine it. It comes from all directions at once, moving like a spiral around a core.

When you practice this visualization for forty-five minutes a day for one week, you may be able to feel the special joyful quality of this healing energy. If you do not contact this feeling at first, try to imagine it, and in time you will feel it. When you do, you no longer see your body; there is only the beautiful white energy filling the open column like milk in a pure crystal glass. Each cell and molecule takes in this healing energy until it is completely saturated.

POINTS 4, 9, and 10:   Measure four finger-widths from the middle of the third point to the fourth. From the fourth point measure four finger-widths down on each side of the head (see Figure 3). Again, a special feeling, almost of pain, indicates the right places. Concentrate on the side-points rather than on the fourth point itself.

Close your eyes, and rub and press point 9 with your left thumb and forefinger, and point 10 with your right thumb and forefinger. Whatever you feel, let yourself actually become that feeling, and go with it wherever it goes. Release the pressure gradually, breathing evenly through both nose and mouth, and allowing your sensations to be distributed throughout your body.

Hold the scalp muscle tightly between thumb and forefinger and rub up an inch and down an inch from the middle of each point. Rubbing these points vigorously will loosen tension in the neck muscles.

POINTS 5, 11, and 12:   Measure four finger-widths from the fourth point to the fifth; from the fifth, measure four finger-widths down on each side to locate the two side-points (see Figure 3). Focus on the two side-points. With your eyes closed, rub these two points slowly with your middle fingers, breathing softly through both nose and mouth. As you rub and press, bring breath, mind, fingers, and sensation so close together that you are no longer sure if you are being massaged by hand, mind, feeling, or breath. Let your awareness and your breath enrich your sensations until they become so full and open-ended they spread beyond your body, stimulating nurturing interactions in the world around you.

POINT 6:   This is the most important of these points. It is located at the back of the neck near the juncture of the skull and the spine, approximately four finger-widths from the center of the fifth point. It may be a little difficult to find at first—it is not in the same place on everyone. If you cannot find it the first time, you will find it another, particularly if you work regularly with the pressure points on your head and face.

You can approach this point by rocking your head gently back and forth, with your eyes closed. Support your forehead with one hand, and with two or three fingers of the other hand press at the back of your neck near the base of the skull. The spot you are looking for can be anywhere within two or three inches of the top of the spine. Perhaps you will find an edge or corner that will lead you to a very sensitive area. You may feel a tiny cracking inside. There is a special energy at this point, a deep kind of pain that is easily transformed into pleasure. Sometimes it seems like an extremely delicious feeling. When your rubbing produces any special or strange feeling, then you have found the right place.

Expand this feeling as much as you can. Inhale a little more deeply, and let the exhalation flow gently. Discontinue rocking your head, but continue to manipulate the point; work with it as if it had four corners, each of which you can press and rub. Relax your stomach, and let your body be still and calm. Imagine that you are flying and that your body is light and airy. Go deeply into the feeling. Sometimes this feeling can be so deep and sensitive that you feel you want to cry. Distribute the feeling all the way down your spine to the sacrum.

This deep feeling brings all of the subtle senses alive. Many tensions become caught in this place and rubbing it refreshes all bodily energies. Feeling washes through the spine and the backs of the shoulders, sometimes reaching the heart.

POINTS 1 and 6: Simultaneously rub and press the first and sixth points, concentrating lightly on the sixth. It does not matter if you cannot find the exact place of the sixth point. Even if the two points are not connected in a direct line, simultaneously pressing these two areas stimulates a special energy which relieves various sensitive blockages.

Close your eyes, and rub the two points strongly with equal pressure for about thirty seconds. Then release the pressure slowly, sit very still, and concentrate loosely on the back of your head and neck. Feel the energies moving through your forehead, perhaps above the eyeballs, to the back of your head and spine. If you do not feel anything, tighten the eyeballs a little, keeping your eyes closed. Then slowly loosen them, and notice any sensations in the back of the neck or head. Perhaps there is a sensation of heat, or a warm and blissful feeling. Sometimes you can almost feel the neck muscles becoming warm and light. There is a gentle quality to this warmth, like touching the body of a tiny new baby. Feel it more, concentrating loosely on the back of your neck and sensing the feelings flowing down your spine and perhaps into your heart.

If you want to develop this particular massage, practice it for forty-five minutes a day for at least two weeks. If possible, practice twice a day.

POINTS 13 and 14:   These points are approximately one inch to each side of the sixth point, along the base of the skull. Use your middle fingers and gradually develop strong pressure as you rub these points.

POINTS 15 and 16:   These points are approximately one inch from points 13 and 14, toward the ear and down a little, near the tip of the mastoid process. Use your middle fingers to experiment with different degrees of pressure on these points.

Neck Massage

As your neck becomes more relaxed, your head and heart become more integrated, and you feel more.

☆ With your middle fingers, find the bumps in the skull just behind your ears, and begin to stroke down the neck muscle. (Use your left hand on the left side, and your right hand on the right side.) You may want to use two fingers. Stroke, rub, and press down this muscle, the sterno-mastoid, following it down your neck to your shoulder. Then return to the bump behind your ear and begin again.

Near the shoulder, the muscle separates into two strands. See if you can feel this slight separation, and as you massage, try to widen it a little. Press the point where the muscle separates with your middle fingers, gradually increasing and decreasing the pressure. Continue massaging this muscle for at least ten minutes. Also try massaging the muscle on the left side of your neck with your right hand; then use your left hand on the right side of your neck. Explore different degrees of pressure, remembering always to release the pressure very slowly.

☆ Press the sterno-mastoid muscle between your thumb and four fingers, working up and down the muscle in this way. Then clasp your hands behind your neck and knead this muscle with the heels of your palms. Breathe softly and evenly through both nose and mouth as you massage, and bring your awareness to the breath. Let the gentle influence of the breath permeate the tensions in your muscles and mind, releasing nurturing feelings.

☆ Using the first and middle fingers of your left hand, slowly knead, press, and stroke down the muscles along the left side of the back of your neck. Then use your right hand to do the same for the muscles on the right side of the back of your neck. Let relaxation expand, unifying body awareness, mental awareness, and breath awareness.

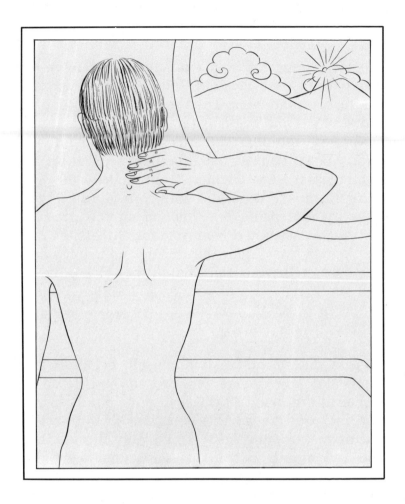

☆ With the index or middle finger of one hand, press just above the large vertebra at the base of the neck. (There is a large bump there on a line with the shoulders.) Slowly move your head back and then press the point strongly. Your finger should be able to go in quite deeply. Release the pressure slowly. Then slowly move your head forward and again press the point strongly. Release the pressure gradually, breathing gently. Slowly lift your head.

☆ Massage the left side of the back of your neck with
your left hand, stroking in from the sides toward the
center-back of your neck in a slightly upward direction. Then repeat on the right side with your right
hand. Keep your head up and your chin in as you do
this.

☆ This is a turning movement from the front to the
back of the neck. Place your right hand under your

chin with the heel of the hand near the hollow of the throat and the fingers and thumb curving around the right side of the neck. Keep your chin up. Slowly glide your right hand around to the right and slightly up to the center-back of your neck. Your whole palm and all your fingers touch your neck; thumb and fingers are together.

As your right hand moves around your neck, place your left hand under your chin, thumb and fingers together pointing to the right, and slowly follow the path of the right hand. As you complete the turning movement with the left hand, begin again with the right. Continue to develop the movement until it becomes smooth.

Change the position of your hands and in the same way, massage the left side of your neck.

☆ Bend your head so your right ear moves toward your right shoulder. Pass first your left hand, fingers pointing up, and then your right hand, up the left side of your neck along a line from the base of your throat just above the breast bone, to the area just behind the ear, and along the base of your skull to the center of the back of your head. You will be following the contours of the sterno-cleido-mastoid muscle. Continue this massage for several minutes, developing a smooth and steady stroking motion with your hands.

As you stroke, breathe gently and evenly through both nose and mouth. Let the breath melt the outlines of hand and neck, merging them together. Gently end the stroke; then bend your head toward your left shoulder and continue the massage on the right side of your neck.

☆ In this stroke, you alternate between massaging your throat and the back of your neck. Encircle the base of your throat with your right hand, the thumb and fingers on either side of the throat. Hold the throat firmly, almost tightly. Place the left hand on the back of your neck, thumb and fingers together, the heel of your hand on the left side of the neck, and your fingers curved around to the right side.

Begin the massage by stroking slowly up your

throat with your right hand, opening your mouth slightly as you stroke. Use your full hand for this massage, all of the palm and fingers touching the skin. Stroke up your throat and up under your chin—lifting your chin as you stroke under it—until your hand moves off the edge of your jaw bone. As you do this, support your head with your left hand.

Then return your right hand to the base of your throat, and support your head from the front as you begin to stroke up the back of your neck with your left hand. Your head will bend forward as you stroke. Continue just past the base of the skull and then return your left hand to the base of your neck and begin again to stroke up your throat with the right hand. Let the massage be very soft, gentle, and calm, and allow yourself to feel the sensations generated throughout your whole body. Do the complete stroke at least three times.

☆ Place your hands at the back of your neck along the base of the skull with your fingers pointing toward each other. Slowly move across the muscles, stroking out from the spine to the sides of your neck. Use the thumbs as well as the fingers. Press strongly as you stroke.

When you reach the sides, bring your hands back to your spine and repeat the movement, a little lower than the first time. By the third time, you will have moved crosswise over the full length of your neck. Continue the massage for several minutes, breathing gently through both nose and mouth, expanding your feelings and sensations. Relax your belly and the area around your eyes.

☆ Place both hands around your neck with the thumbs under your chin and your fingers at the back of your neck. Slowly stroke down the length of the neck, with as complete contact between your hands and your neck as possible. Continue at least a minute.

☆ Place your right hand under your chin, with the thumb and middle finger on the muscles on either side of your throat and the rest of your hand in as much contact with your neck as possible. Open your mouth slightly, and lift your chin a little. Very slowly stroke down your neck. Begin to stroke with your left hand as soon as there is room under your chin. Stroke down the front of your neck with one hand following the other so closely that the second stroke begins before the first one ends. Continue, alternating hands, for several minutes, breathing gently through both nose and mouth.

You may want to do the neck massage, or portions of the massage, at various times throughout the day —whenever you feel tense. Difficult situations and problems always seem to catch us when there is the least time to deal with them. Tension builds up, often settling in the neck, as well as in the musculature where the neck meets the shoulders and the head.

When you are feeling especially tense, notice if you are holding tension in your neck. Although you may feel as if you do not have the time to spare, relax for a few minutes. Slowly begin to rub your neck. You may wish to rub very lightly at first. Lightly concentrate on soothing feelings spreading from your neck down your spine, into all your limbs. Let warm, nurturing sensations spread up into your head as well. These feelings will lighten your whole body, and heal tension in your mind, so that you can think more clearly. When the mind and body are relaxed, both work better; problems take care of themselves, and your days become much lighter and easier.

Shoulder Massage

Our shoulders are often tense with unexpressed feelings. When we gently release these tensions, feeling flows more smoothly between the chest and neck, and between the front and back of the body.

☆ If you are pregnant or have had any kind of neck injury, omit the head rotation in this massage.

Cross your arms and rest your hands on the opposite shoulder, close to your neck. Keeping your hands in this position, use your middle fingers to massage your shoulder muscle in a circular movement. (There is a point here which is shown in Figure 9 on page 141.) Move the fingers very slowly, pressing strongly. As you do this, very slowly rotate your head clockwise, with your eyes closed, breathing softly through both nose and mouth. Coordinate the two movements. After three clockwise rotations, make three counter-clockwise rotations. Remember to move very slowly and to breathe gently and evenly through both nose and mouth. Release the pressure slowly as the rotations come to an end. Sit quietly for a few minutes.

☆ Press with the middle and index fingers of one hand on the back of the opposite shoulder near the arm, where the bone of the shoulder blade divides. (This point is shown in Figure 9.) As you press, slowly rotate your shoulder first in one direction, then the other, gently breathing through nose and mouth. Increase and decrease the pressure gradually. Repeat the massage on the other shoulder.

☆ In whatever way seems best to you, massage your shoulders, working over the top of the shoulder and down the shoulder blades, moving toward the spine. Then work back up to the top of the shoulder, using pinching and rotating movements. The powerful trapezius muscle which covers the shoulder and upper back holds many tensions, even pain; work slowly with knots and tender areas until they become more relaxed. Spend at least ten minutes on this massage.

Chest Massage

Massaging the chest improves breathing and circulation, and helps to open the heart to feeling. It is especially common for women to hold tension in this area.

☆ Using one or two fingers, slowly press along the collarbone from the base of your neck out to your shoulder. Then press along and between each rib of

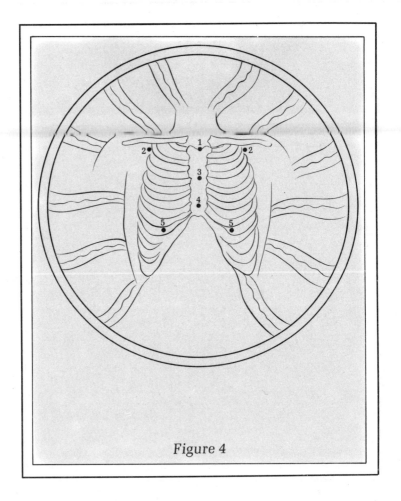

Figure 4

the chest from the breastbone to the side of your
chest and where possible, under your arm. There are
many sensitive points along these paths. Work thoroughly in a meditative way, breathing into the area
you are massaging. Pay particular attention to points
1–5 in Figure 4. (Point 1 is just above the breastbone;
point 4 is the midpoint between the nipples; and point
3 is midway between points 1 and 4.)

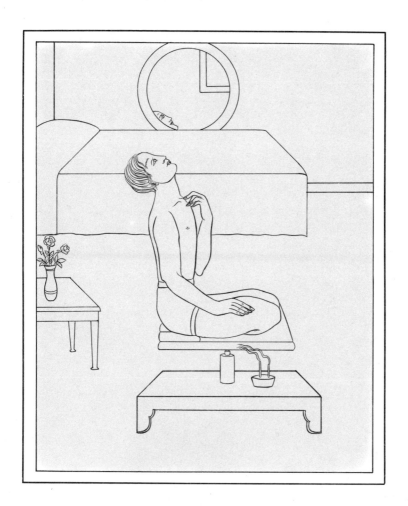

☆   Press the point just above the breastbone (point 1 in Figure 4) with your index finger or thumb, and as you do so, arch your spine and neck backward, but without straining. Do not let your head go all the way back. Hold for a minute, continuing to press strongly. Breathe gently through both nose and mouth. Then very slowly release the pressure, and straighten your spine and neck.

☆ This massage is for both the chest and the belly. Place your left hand at the base of your throat, the thumb and fingers on either side of the throat, and place your right hand on the left side of your waist. Make sure both hands are in full contact with your body. Very slowly and firmly, simultaneously glide your left hand down over your chest and belly to your left waist, and your right hand up your belly and chest to the base of your neck. Your hands will move along parallel paths, in opposite directions. Then in the same way, without stopping, move your right hand down to the left side of your waist as you move your left hand up to the base of your throat. Continue this massage for several minutes, developing a steady rhythm, and paying attention to any feelings that arise. Join your feelings to the breath; then bring them into the massage and let them deepen the quality of the rhythm.

End the stroke in a gentle way; then place your right hand at the base of your throat, and your left hand on the right side of your waist, and continue the massage for several minutes on the right side of your body.

☆ Place your right hand near the top of your left shoulder and your left hand near the top of your right shoulder. Keeping both palms in contact with your chest at all times, simultaneously move the two hands toward each other and then away from each other. Move them slowly and rhythmically back and forth until you have covered the entire surface of your chest. Continue for at least one minute, breathing gently through both nose and mouth.

☆ Place your hands flat on the sides of your body, as close under your armpits as possible, with the fingers pointing down. This may be a little difficult at first. Pressing firmly, slowly move your hands down your sides to your hips. Let the contact between your hands and your body be as full as possible. Breathe softly through both nose and mouth. Continue for several minutes.

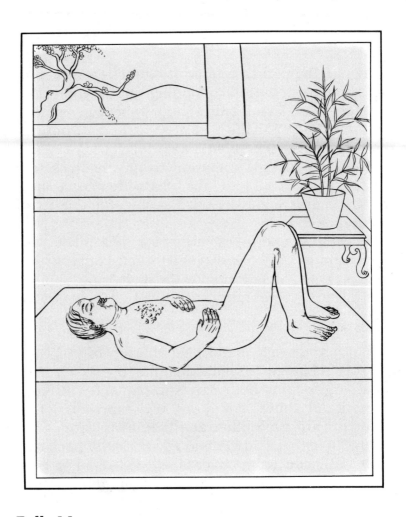

Belly Massage

When the belly truly relaxes, we become free from grasping. Massage here is especially important for men since it is common for men to hold tension in this area.

☆ This massage is best done in the evening, at least one hour after eating, and without clothes. Lie down on your back with your eyes closed. Separate your legs a comfortable distance, bend your knees and draw your feet toward your body a little. Relax your belly. Place your right hand on your lower abdomen and your left hand on your upper abdomen. Let the contact between your hands and your belly be as full as possible. Slowly begin to massage in a large circle, moving your right hand up on the right side of your belly and your left hand down on the left side. When the left hand crosses over the right arm, let the touch between hand and arm be as complete as possible.

At first massage with very light pressure; gradually develop medium and finally, strong pressure. Press especially deeply on the left side. Then decrease the pressure, passing gradually through each stage until the pressure is so light you are not sure your hand is touching your belly at all. Take at least five minutes for this massage. This motion follows the curvature of the large intestine.

☆ Gradually move one hand to the upper border of your belly and the other to the lower border, near the pubic bone. Place the edges of your hands against your body, so the palms face each other. Hold your breathe a little, but not very intensely. Slowly push down with the upper hand and up with the lower hand, making your belly into a ball. Be very relaxed in the upper part of your body, especially your chest and neck. Remember to hold the breath. Exhale slowly, then repeat several times.

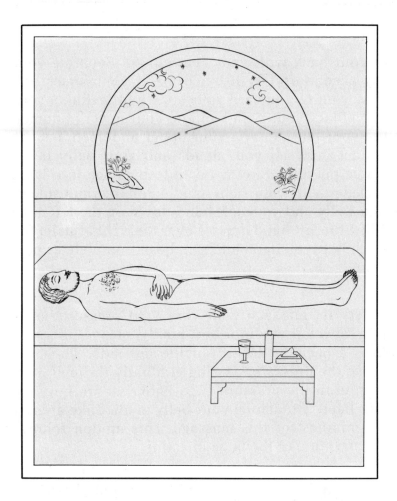

☆ Place your left hand on your belly, with the fingers pointing to the right. Push your belly out a little and keep it there, breathing gently through nose and mouth. With your hand in place, develop a slow circular movement with the edge of the hand and the tips of the fingers, pressing deeply into the belly, especially on the left side. Continue for several minutes creating a steady rhythm, joining the rhythm to the breath.

☆ Now in any way that feels appropriate to you, continue to massage the superficial musculature of your belly area. Massage up on the right side of your abdomen, across the area under the ribs to the left, and down on the left side. Then massage more deeply, gently kneading all of your internal organs and tissues, starting under the ribs and working down into the pelvic area. Again, work down on the left side and up on the right. When you find a tense place, spend more time there. Breathe easily, and let the breath soften and melt the edges of your tension. Allow the breath to pass into the very center of the tension, carrying soothing feelings which calm and nurture you.

When you feel ready to stop, repetition of the first stroke in this section—simultaneous circling movements with both hands—will create a natural conclusion. Then lie quietly for a few minutes, breathing gently through both nose and mouth.

When you are away from home, perhaps in a tense or emotional situation that is giving you difficulty, the belly massage can be particularly helpful. You may find that it produces feelings of deep relaxation which flow outward from your belly, affecting your whole outlook, enabling you to think clearly and act effectively. What appeared to be unpleasant may even become enjoyable. You can do the belly massage even when it is not convenient for you to lie down. To do it in a sitting position, support your lower back with one hand and rub the belly with the other hand. When you rub in circles, be sure to rub up on the right and down on the left.

☆   You can also do the following massage in a sitting position: strongly press the navel (there is a pressure point there) with the middle finger of one hand while arching your spine and neck backward. Do not let your head go all the way back. Rest the other hand on your knee. Hold for a minute, breathing gently through nose and mouth. Then slowly straighten your spine while gradually decreasing the pressure. Explore the feelings generated by the massage.

Arm Massage

Massaging the arms improves both breathing and circulation so they become rhythmic and balanced. Muscles throughout the body are strengthened, and a fresh pure quality is stimulated within the subtle energies.

☆ Massage your forearm in rings the width of your hand. To do this, grasp your left wrist with the right hand so that thumb and middle finger meet at the inside of the wrist. Slowly turn your right hand in one direction until you have made as complete a ring as possible. Massage firmly, squeezing and pressing the arm as you turn your hand. Then shift your hand up your arm one hand-width, and turn your hand in the other direction to make the second ring. By the fourth ring you will be up to or a little beyond the elbow.

☆   The rest of the forearm massage is oriented to the pressure points illustrated in Figure 5. Massaging these points will generate many flavors of feeling.

To find the first point, bend your left arm at the elbow so your hand points to the ceiling. On the back of your upper arm, measure the width of three fingers up from the point of the elbow (in the direction of the armpit). Press strongly on this point with your right forefinger. Straighten your neck a little as you press. Then slowly stretch out your left arm in front of you, palm up, and continue to press and manipulate this point. Take time to experience what you feel. Then slowly work down the length of the back of the arm to the wrist, as if drawing a straight line from this point. Slowly rub and press as you move down the arm. When you feel a little pain or find a sensitive spot, spend more time there. You may eventually be able to locate specific nerves in your arm.

Find the first point again, and then measure from it approximately two finger-widths to the left and two finger-widths to the right. These are the next two points. The second point is toward the inside of the arm; the third point is toward the outside of the arm.

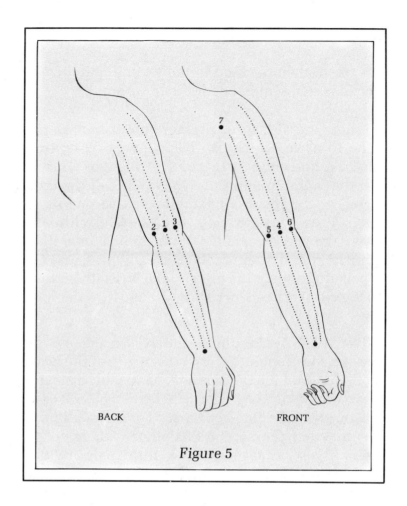

BACK

FRONT

Figure 5

Both points are on the back of the upper arm. Once you find these points, mentally divide the back of your arm into three sections lengthwise, picturing a line from each point running from behind the elbow to the back of the wrist. Straighten your arm, and begin to press the second point gently and steadily. Slowly develop more pressure; and finally, press strongly. When you release the pressure, do so gradually. Then slowly work your way down the imagined line to your wrist, then back up to the second point. Do the same massage sequence for the third point.

☆   There are also three pressure points on the front of the forearm which can be followed down to the wrist. To find the fourth point, straighten your arm with the palm up and press the middle of the crease or ring at the inside of the elbow. Use one or two fingers. Press very strongly. Then slowly, without releasing the pressure, move down an imagined line to the inside of your wrist. Exert steady pressure. Give special attention to the point at the wrist (this is point 1 in Figure 1). Then work slowly back up to the fourth point.

The fifth point is approximately two finger-widths from the fourth point toward the inside of the arm. If you do not find it exactly there, bend your arm at the elbow and place a finger where the elbow-crease ends on the inside of your arm. Then straighten the arm and exert pressure at this point with one or two fingers. This point may be a little painful. Press deeply into the muscle. Then slowly work down the imagined line to the wrist. Press a little strongly, allowing the sensations you feel to expand. Throughout the massage breathe gently and easily through both nose and mouth. Slowly work back up to the fifth point.

The sixth point is about two finger-widths from the first point, toward the outside of the arm. This point may be the most sensitive of the three. Slowly press the point, rubbing forward and back and to the sides. As you continue to rub slowly, pay attention to the quality of the feelings generated. Rubbing here may release sensations in your heart area, your neck, and possibly, your intestines. Slowly work down the imagined line to the wrist. When you reach the wrist, go a little beyond the farthest wrist-crease. There is a special place next to the bone. Press there with your fingers, one at a time, keeping your arm almost straight. Then slowly massage back up to the sixth point, being especially aware of sensations in your heart area.

Be sure to do the complete forearm massage on both arms.

☆ Now massage the upper arm in rings from elbow to shoulder. (See the first forearm massage above.)

Massage from each of the three pressure points on the back of the arm up to the top of the shoulder and down again to the elbow. Do the same for the three pressure points on the front of the arm.

Gently massage the deltoid muscle over the shoulder cap and the biceps muscle on the front of the upper arm until they have no knots or sore areas in them. These muscles both tend to become overdeveloped in men. There should be a continuous flow from one muscle to the next, yet each individual muscle should be able to move alone.

Rest your hand on your knee, and straighten your arm as you gently massage the biceps with the other hand. Straightening the arm will help to increase the length and freedom of the biceps.

Be sure to do the complete upper arm massage on both arms.

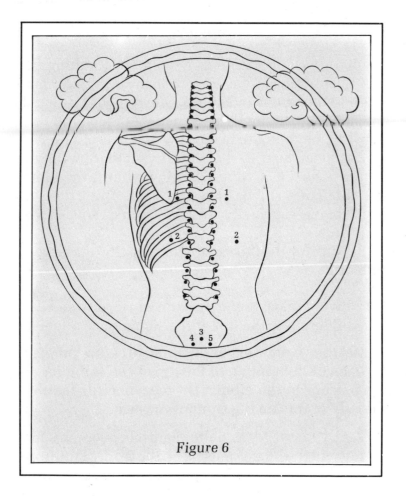

Figure 6

Back Massage

Massaging the back helps to release feelings of joy and love, and gives life and strength to all the senses.

☆ Start at the side of your chest, in the armpit, and massage toward the center of your back. There are large muscles in this area, so take your time and massage them thoroughly. Work around and on top

of the shoulder blades. Do first one side of the back,
then the other.

☆ There are two pressure points just above the
lower curve of the shoulder blades (points 1 in Figure
6). Press these points with your middle fingers, either
at the same time or separately. Experiment to find
what works best for you. Slowly increase and decrease the pressure.

☆ Points 2 in Figure 6 are on the muscle at about the
level of the kidneys, and are exactly opposite chest
points 5 (see Figure 4). Press both of these back points
with your middle fingers, gradually developing
strong pressure. Release slowly. Then use one middle
finger to press one back point, and the other to press
the corresponding chest point. Go deeply into the
sensations stimulated by pressure on both points.
Then do the other pair of points.

☆ With your thumbs, press the three points on the
sacrum (points 3, 4, and 5 in Figure 6), gradually increasing and decreasing the pressure. Using your
thumbs wherever possible—and your middle fingers
when your thumbs cannot reach—strongly press the
points between the vertebrae, working from the base
of the spine all the way up to the base of the skull.

☆ Lie on your back on a mat or soft rug. Separate
your legs a comfortable distance, bend your knees,
and place your feet flat on the floor. Raise your pelvis
up from the floor, shifting your weight toward your
shoulders. With both hands massage around the
sides of your body toward the back.

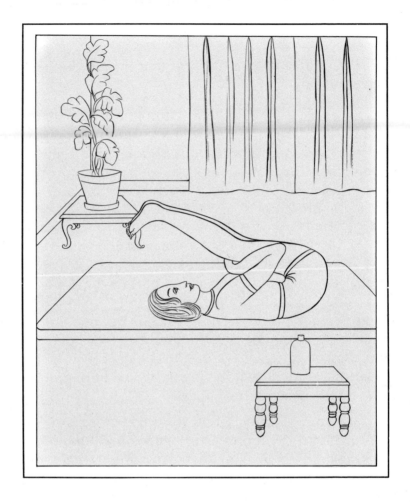

☆ The following backward roll will massage the upper area of your back where your hands cannot reach. Sit with your legs a comfortable distance apart, your knees bent, and your feet flat on the floor. Hold your left knee with your left hand and your right knee with your right hand. Without moving your legs, slowly lean backward until your arms become straight and the small of your back is as close as possible to the floor. Then slowly draw your feet along the floor toward you and roll backward, straightening your legs. Roll forward to return to the sitting position. Be sure the small of your back touches the floor during the roll. Do the roll several times.

☆ Roll backward in the manner described above, and stay on your back. Draw your knees close to your chest, put your arms around your knees, and roll from side to side a little, massaging your back as fully as possible. Roll slowly and gently for a short distance, but not so far that you lose your balance.

This massage, and the backward roll massage, will relieve tension throughout the whole length of the spine. As the muscles alongside the spine relax and lengthen, sensations of well-being and joy are released. Nurture yourself with these feelings; let them touch you inside your heart. As you do these massages, move so gently and softly that your body loses a sense of definite form: you become part of the feeling of joy. Your sensation is not captured in just one corner of your body; it spreads to every part. This sensation can become so large and full that it extends beyond your body, and you become part of a universal sensation. The boundaries between you and the world around you dissolve.

☆ Now lie on your stomach and massage the sides of your body and your back, moving your hands toward the center of your back. It feels good to use the knuckles in this area.

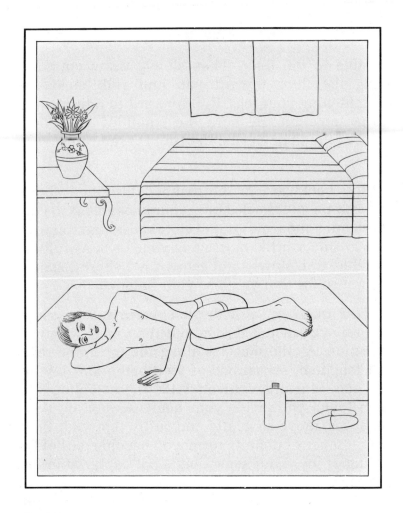

Hip Massage

Massaging the hip helps to stimulate feelings and energies that become blocked from lack of exercise.

☆ Lie down on the floor on your right side with your legs fairly straight, your left leg in front of the right. Start at the waist, and use both hands to massage the left hip and buttock in the direction of the leg. Try

massaging with your fists too. Small circular movements with the knuckles will help to loosen tension.
If you discover any sensitive areas, massage thoroughly there, merging the breath with your sensations, and opening the feeling of relaxation as wide as
you can. If you do not feel much sensation at first,
simply continue to bring your breath and your awareness into the massage; then sensation can awaken
within you. Continue with the next part of this massage before massaging your right side.

☆ Tuck one arm under your head as a pillow, and
place the other hand flat on the ground near your
chest. Straighten your legs and rest your left leg on
top of your right. Slowly lift both legs six inches or so
above the ground. Without lowering your legs, bend
your knees, pressing the calves as close to the thighs
as you can. Hold briefly, and then bring your knees
close to your chest. Be aware of the pressure of your
right hip against the floor. Now slowly straighten your
legs, lower them gently to the floor, and rest. Repeat
slowly two times.

Explore the feelings generated by the massage.
Feel the flow of energy from your hip to your legs and
feet; then feel the flow of sensation to the upper part
of your body as well. Instead of feeling the sensations
in your hip, feel the sensations in the rest of your
body. By massaging your hip you can spread healing
and invigorating feelings throughout your whole
system.

Now roll onto your left side and repeat the two
parts of this massage on the right side.

Leg Massage

Lack of exercise prevents the flow of feeling in our legs as well as our hips, and massage here can begin to awaken sleeping energies. When you exercise regularly, massaging the legs can smooth the flow of sensation, and relieve subtle blockages.

☆ Sit on a mat or cushion with your left knee bent, and your left foot flat on the floor. Rub between the

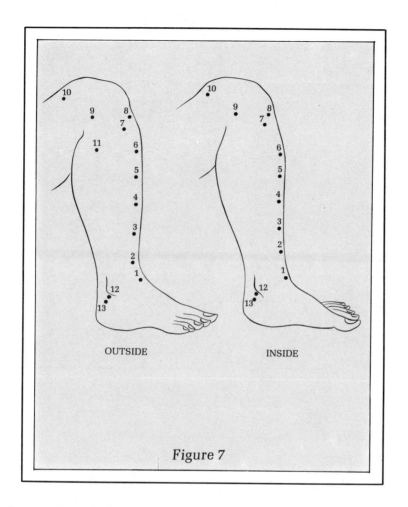

OUTSIDE

INSIDE

Figure 7

big toe and the second toe, and trace between the
tendons up to the ankle. Continue up the shinbone to
the knee, with thumb and forefinger on either side of
the bone. Press pressure points 1–6 along here as
indicated in Figure 7. If you find small clusters of
tension or pain, return at intervals to rub them in
small circles until any knots loosen and perhaps dissolve. Breathe gently through both nose and mouth as
you rub. Repeat the massage for the right leg.

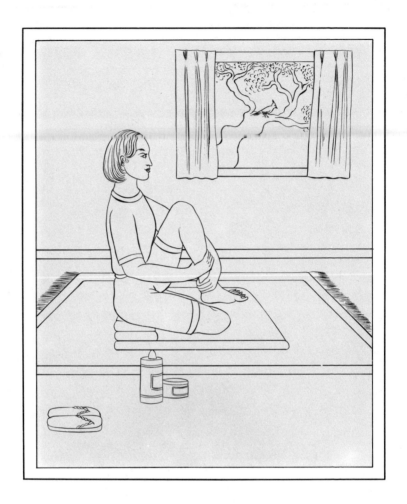

☆ With both hands grasp your leg just above the ankle, one hand above the other, thumbs at the back of the leg. Simultaneously twist and press both hands right, then left, as you work up the shin to the knee-cap. Hold your leg firmly as you twist, letting the contact between hands and leg be as complete as possible.

Change the position of your hands so the thumbs are on the front of the shin, and repeat the leg twist.

☆ Massage around the knee, the four corners of the kneecap, at the sides of the knee, and behind the knee. Using your thumbs, press the four sets of points (points 7–10) on and around the knee at the locations pictured in Figure 7. If you do not find these points at first, do not give up; you will find them as you go deeper into your feelings and let them guide you. Breathe evenly through nose and mouth as you explore with your fingers. When you find a point, experiment with degrees of pressure; release the pressure slowly.

☆ Press strongly with your thumb on the point approximately five and a half inches down from the top of the kneecap on the outside of the leg. Release the pressure very slowly.

☆ To massage the thigh muscles, place one hand on the back and one hand on the front of the thigh. Rub from side to side in large, sweeping movements, pressing as strongly as you can. Make certain your whole palm is in contact with your leg as you rub. Move both hands in the same direction; then move them in opposite directions. Then place one hand on the inside and one hand on the outside of the thigh and continue the movements. Also explore for any knots or painful places by tracing the muscles up from the knee area with your fingers. Give a circular rub with four fingers to any tense places you find. Pay special attention to the places where the thigh muscles join the hip and knee.

☆ Now reverse the position of your legs, and repeat the leg massage for the right leg.

☆ Sit with your legs outstretched in front of you, and lightly place your palms flat on the floor near your hips. Relax your legs as much as you can. Bend your right knee, and place the pad of the foot high up on the left leg, near the groin. Use the right leg and foot to massage the left leg, curling around it and moving up and down its entire length and around the sides. Continue for several minutes. Then change the position of the legs and use the left leg to massage the right.

Foot Massage

Like massaging the hands, massaging the feet can tune and vitalize the whole body.

☆ Sit on a mat or cushion with your back straight and your legs loosely crossed, the left leg outside the right. Lift your left knee, interlace your fingers and use them to support the ball of your left foot. Push your foot against your hands, straightening the leg in front of you as much as possible. Feel the stretch in your leg and the ball of your foot, and hold briefly. Then slowly lower your leg to the floor. Repeat for the right leg and foot.

☆ Cross the left leg over the right, resting the left shin on the right thigh. Support the foot with your right hand on the heel and grasp the toes in your left hand. Vigorously rotate the toes in a circle, first in one direction and then in the other. Then extend the circles so you are rotating the ball of the foot as well as the toes. The whole upper part of the foot can participate in these circles. Vary the rhythm, rotating both slowly and quickly.

☆ Still grasping all the toes with the left hand, bend them back and forth several times. Then extend the motion so the ball of the foot as well as the toes bends back and forth. The foot is very relaxed during this movement.

☆ Now begin to massage the toes of the left foot, using the fingers of both hands. Apply pressure to the pads of the toes. Then massage each toe, one at a time, from the base of the toe to the pad. Be sure to massage the sides as well as the front and back of each toe. Direct pressure as well as rotating motions may be used. Pull gently on each toe to stretch it.

☆ Massage the areas where the toes join the sole, using the thumb or knuckle. Press the four pairs of points between the bones pictured in Figure 8 (points

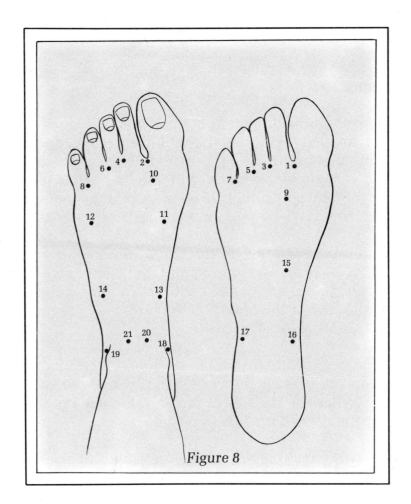

Figure 8

1–8), using the thumb on the sole, and the middle finger on the top of the foot.

☆ Move to the ball of the foot; using the thumbs of both hands, strongly probe each joint. Press deeply between the pads of the ball of the foot. There is no danger of harming yourself, so do not hesitate to press as hard as you like. When you find a sensitive place, trace it briefly, and become acquainted with it. Touching certain sensitive places may release memories.

☆ Give special attention to point 9 in the pad of the foot immediately behind the bulge of the big toe, using medium to strong pressure. Release the pressure very slowly. With your thumb on point 9, place your forefinger on point 10 on the top of the foot, and work these two points simultaneously.

☆ With the thumbs on the ball of the foot, use the fingers to press the top of the foot. Then move the thumbs to the instep and continue rotating pressure on all parts of the top of the foot. Include points 11, 12, 13, and 14 (see Figure 8).

☆ Now return to the sole of the foot. Use the knuckles and the fist of the right hand to exert pressure everywhere on the sole of the foot. Include point 15, in the middle of the sole (see Figure 8).

☆ With your thumbs, stroke the length of the sole diagonally, starting just in front of the heel on the inside of the foot. Alternate your thumbs, creating a continuous sweeping rhythm. It is important not to break the contact between hand and foot during this part of the massage. Then stroke diagonally from the side near the heel to the ball of the big toe. You may feel different feeling-tones, some of them slightly painful. Breathe into the pain, and let it deepen into nurturing sensation as you exhale. Stroke very slowly, sensing fully, with your belly relaxed. Let the breath and the stroke become unified with sensation.

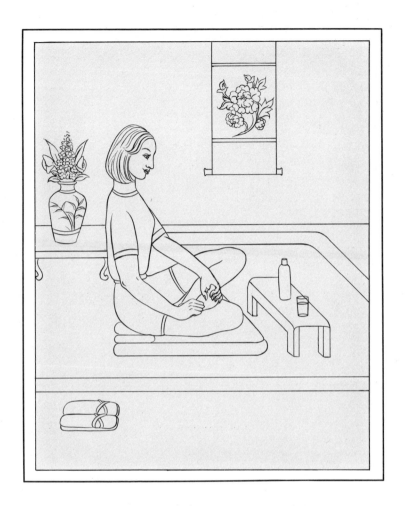

☆ Arch the toes back with your left hand and jut the heel forward. A valley is formed in the middle of the sole when you do this. Using the knuckles or fist of your right hand, press firmly all the points along this valley. The tendon here may be very tight and sore. You may feel a sudden surge of energy or a rush of warmth around your heart as you press. Explore sensitively, bringing your awareness into whatever you feel.

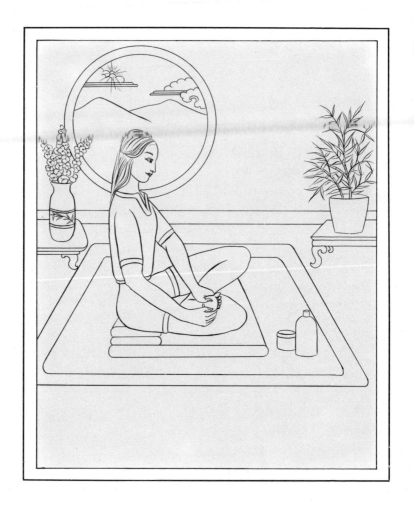

☆ Grasp one side of the ball of the foot with the left hand and the other side with the right hand. Pull apart as though you were trying to make the sole convex. Maximize the contact of your hands and feet as you pull. Then pull the sides of the feet toward you as if trying to make the sole concave.

☆ Move to the heel; pinch and probe all areas. Strongly press points 16 and 17 (see Figure 8).

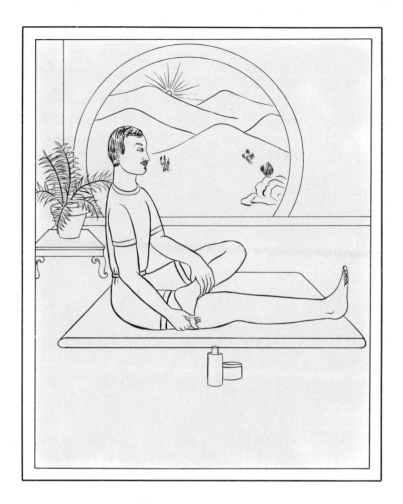

☆ Grasp the toes of the left foot with your right hand and rest your left hand on the left leg just above the ankle. With your foot relaxed, slowly rotate the ankle in a circle, first in one direction, and then in the other. Let your hand do the work; your foot is completely relaxed. If you feel a tight place, explore it by moving more slowly, breathing gently. Let tensions relax throughout your body. Continue the rotations for several minutes, until they become smooth and easy.

☆ Pinch and rub vigorously the Achilles' tendon at the back of the foot.

☆ Apply pressure to all points on and around the ankle. Include ankle points 12 and 13 in Figure 7, and points 18–21 in Figure 8. (Figure 7 is on p. 129.)

☆ Position your foot so you can massage the top of it comfortably. Rub between the toes and trace between the tendons, working up to the ankle. Include the sides of the foot in your massage.

☆ Repeat the foot massage, this time a little more slowly. If there are any points at which pressure produces any changes in feeling, continue to apply pressure and try to go into the feeling, expanding it as much as possible. If the massage uncovers a sore spot, massage it gently without lingering over it.

Now try this simple test. Stand up, resting your weight equally on each foot. How do the two feet relate to the ground? Do you notice any differences? Does one foot feel light, the other heavy? Does there seem to be an energy, an aliveness quality in one foot in contrast to dullness in the other?

☆ Now repeat the foot massage on the right foot.

Figure 9 shows all of the pressure points mentioned in this chapter. These pressure points, like all Kum Nye exercises and massages, are a map to guide you in exploring the rich inner treasures of your body, mind, and senses. As you become familiar with these points and the special qualities of feeling which

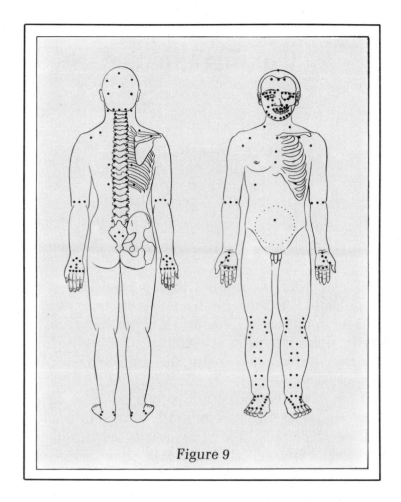

Figure 9

pressure on them produces, your understanding of the nature of embodiment will deepen. You may discover additional pressure points in your explorations (even internal ones). As your practice progresses, you may be able to chart your experiences of body and mind, creating maps which will guide others.

Guiding Practice

*Once you have tasted
inner relaxation, your body will be
your truest guide.*

Exercise that is genuine and pure, uniting body and mind, truly revitalizes our energies and sustains us in our daily lives. We become free from negativity, dissatisfaction, and confusion, for we are able to satisfy ourselves directly, instead of chasing after rainbows.

Kum Nye exercises activate a positive healing process that nurtures us mentally and emotionally as well as physically. These exercises are designed to contact the whole body and mind, and in doing so, to unify all its aspects. They stimulate body awareness, sensory awareness, and mental awareness, affecting not only the physical systems of the body, but the subtle energy and emotional systems as well. Each exercise loosens both physical and psychological tension, and stimulates feelings which lead to both physical and mental balance.

When we give our sensations more flavor, really bringing them into our bodies, we can expand them through our senses and thoughts. When we join breath and awareness to each feeling, it turns into healing, invigorating energy. We may not be able to reach the roots of every feeling at first, but when we make the feelings richer, they grow quickly. If a 'negative' emotion such as resentment or fear arises, we can mix it with our positive sensations and memories, like adding milk to tea. We can make it delicious, give it more flavor, until positive and negative become the same and are equal.

Once the flow of feeling is stimulated, interconnecting all aspects of body and mind, each exercise becomes an opportunity to explore the ease that characterizes the harmonious relationship among body, breath, senses, mind, and environment. The mind and breath support the senses, and the senses support the body, breath, and mind. The body and mind become one.

As our mental and physical energies become vital and sustaining, we grow clear and confident. Our communication becomes more alive. We can live more cheerfully and selflessly, with an ever-increasing capacity for enjoyment. We experience the beauty of natural existence, and can see a dimension of experience that we ordinarily are not able to touch.

Our concentration takes on a light, almost floating quality which opens us to broader perspectives of experience. Our inner cosmos becomes a unity which cannot be separated from the outer cosmos. We realize that there are no separate spaces, and all space becomes open and inviting. As we continue to develop the experience of balance, we develop an open, willing, and accepting attitude toward every aspect of life. All of our actions express a wholesome attitude, and daily life becomes luminous in quality.

This ongoing exercise of body, mind, and senses —this interaction—is embodiment: a living, continuing process of enjoyment that informs all of our activities. As we deeply feel a sensation of inner warmth, thick and rich like fresh cream, a quality of sweetness develops, a deep, gentle quality which continues to increase and refresh itself, fulfilling and nourishing us and those around us. We can expand this quality of enjoyment more and more, until every movement, every word, and every glance becomes a subtle interaction, an exercise.

The ideal way to practice Kum Nye is twice a day, doing the breathing and movement exercises in the morning, and massage in the evening. Two groups of exercises are included here to help you in planning your morning practice during the first few months. (Part 2 of this book contains many more movement exercises.) If you wish to practice only once a day, some massage can easily be added to the movement exercises you choose.

There are ten exercises in each group. (The exercises in Group One correspond in difficulty to those in Stage One of Part 2; the exercises in Group Two correspond to those in Stage Two of Part 2.) You might spend two or three months of practice on each group. To develop the exercises in Group One, you might first choose two or three exercises out of the ten, and practice each one daily for about fifteen minutes. After a few weeks, you could add one or two more exercises, continuing to practice two or three exercises each day.

After developing the exercises in Group One over a period of two or three months, you might then add exercises from Group Two (one or two at a time) rather than change to a whole new set. Once you have tasted inner relaxation, your body will be your truest guide.

Let your body lead you to the exercises you practice. If you are unused to exercising, be especially gentle with yourself, and do not try to do too much. Remember that it is the quality of the movement that is most important. If you are pregnant, do the breathing exercises and the gentle movement exercises such as Exercises 18, 22, 24, and 30. If you have had any kind of neck injury, Exercise 17 is not recommended. If you have had a back injury, it may be best not to do the exercises in which the spine bends forward or backward. Use your own judgment; if you practice any of them, move very gently, with awareness. If you have had an operation within the last three or four months, develop the gentler exercises such as those mentioned above.

When you practice the exercises, move very slowly and smoothly. This will allow you to be sensitive and alert to variations in your feelings and body processes. Always move with awareness—never mechanically or absent-mindedly—so that you develop the quality of the practice. Breathe evenly through both nose and mouth, so your energies are constantly balanced, and your sensations are stimulated within balance. •

Let your senses, feelings, breath, and awareness move in and with your body. Rather than directing your eyes outward, look inward with the eyes of the senses, into feelings or tension. Then gradually sensing will become awareness. Too much seriousness can lead to rigidity, so try to develop a quality in your practice that is a combination of lightness and internal awareness.

As you go deeper into your feelings, your experience of relaxation will continue to expand, and your increasing alertness and capacity for enjoyment will give stability to your life. As your body is nourished by your sensations, you become emotionally more healthy, and an uplifting quality develops within your senses.

Group One

Before beginning these exercises (and at various times as you practice them in the next few months), you may find it useful to reread the chapter, "Preparation." After doing so, read through the exercises in this group, and when you are drawn to one, try it. You may want to try a number of the exercises, but then go back to two or three you especially like, and develop them for a few weeks before adding more. Remember not to rush. Stay with an exercise until it opens the door to your senses, awakening feelings which heal both your body and mind.

Forty-five minutes is a good length of time to practice, although even twenty minutes will bring results. Begin by spending fifteen to twenty minutes on each exercise. Do an exercise three times, and spend two or three minutes or more on each repetition; then sit quietly for five or ten minutes. Later, you may want to practice an exercise for a longer period of time. If you feel strong emotions, sit quietly and relax for a while before exercising. If you do not feel well, be sure not to do too much.

You will find that the exercises in this group release tension in your upper body, especially the shoulders, neck, and head, and in the spine. The stretching exercises such as Exercises 19, 20, and 21 are especially pleasurable to do in the morning. Do not stretch too much or too quickly; this may strain muscles and cause a heavy, inert state of mind. Slowly ease into the stretch, breathing evenly through both nose and mouth, and develop a quality of lightness. Then feeling and energy are redistributed throughout the body, and you will begin to feel more in your heart.

These simple exercises help us develop the abundant riches of our inner resources in a natural way. Even if nothing in particular appears to be happening while you do an exercise, a change will be gradually occurring in the quality of your daily life. Every aspect of experience will become clearer and more vital. Every activity of the senses—smelling, seeing, hearing, tasting—will become more substantial, full, and alive. Life develops a special tangy quality.

Exercise 15   Loosening Up

Sit cross-legged on a mat or cushion with your hands on your knees and your arms straight. Facing forward and breathing easily through both nose and mouth, very slowly move your shoulders so the right shoulder moves forward as far as possible and the left shoulder moves back as far as possible. Keep your right arm straight and let the left elbow bend.

Take about fifteen seconds for this movement. Then slowly move your left shoulder forward as your right shoulder moves back, straightening your left arm and allowing your right elbow to bend. Be sure to face forward, so the shoulders move independently of the head. This will feel a little strange at first, for we are accustomed to moving the head and shoulders together. Move very slowly, sensing the feelings awakened in your body. Feel the stretch in your back and neck at the end of the movement; you may feel sensations of warmth there.

Do the complete movement, first one side, then the other, three or nine times. Then sit quietly in the sitting posture for five to ten minutes, distributing the sensations awakened by this movement to your whole body, and beyond, to the surrounding universe.

This exercise relaxes the upper back, especially the muscles of the shoulder blades. It also relaxes the hips.

Exercise 16   Touching Feeling

Sit cross-legged on a mat or cushion with your hands
on your knees. Relax your belly. Inhale and slowly
lift your shoulders as high as possible, allowing the
position of your hands to shift as needed. When you
think your shoulders are as high as they can go, relax
while still holding them up, and you may find they
can be raised a little more. Let your neck settle down
between your shoulders.

Now hold your breath a little and lightly imagine the back of your neck, as if it were fresh and warm like that of a happy baby.... Then very slowly exhale, and in very slow motion, rotate your shoulders back and down, feeling the sensations in the back of your neck and spine. Keep your belly relaxed. Let your hands and arms be very relaxed—you may feel sensations of warmth and softness there. Slowly continue to rotate your shoulders—forward, up, back, and down—three or nine times. Spend at least one minute on each rotation. Then find a place in the movement where you can comfortably change direction, and make three or nine rotations the other way. At the end, sit in the sitting posture for five to ten minutes, expanding your sensations and feelings.

This exercise can also be done standing. Let your arms hang relaxed and close to your body as you rotate your shoulders in the shoulder joints.

Exercise 17   Lightening Thoughts

If you are pregnant or have had any kind of neck
injury, it is best not to do this exercise. Do it especially slowly if your neck muscles are tight. Throughout the exercise breathe very slowly and evenly
through both nose and mouth. This is important, for
if the breathing is too fast or uneven, this exercise
can produce effects such as nausea or disorientation.

Sit cross-legged on a mat or cushion with your hands on your knees. With your mouth slightly open, breathing gently, very slowly lower your chin toward your chest; then very slowly lift the chin until it points toward the ceiling. Repeat this very slow lifting and lowering of the chin several times.

Now very slowly, move your head so your right ear moves in the direction of your right shoulder, and then so your left ear moves in the direction of your left shoulder. Repeat several times.

Softly close your eyes and slowly begin to rotate your head clockwise, as if drawing a perfect circle with the top of the head. Relax your shoulders—they should not move with the head. Let the neck muscles open and lengthen, without stretching too much. Make the circle as large and full as you can without straining—let the ears come close to the shoulders and the chin near the chest. When you come to a tight or painful place, move your head back and forth very slowly, allowing the muscles to loosen and lengthen. You may catch a thought related to the tightness. Slow the speed of the rotation down with mind, breath, and senses until the movement is almost imperceptible. Be aware of your whole body, even your toes and fingertips.

During the rotation, concentrate loosely on the juncture of your skull and spine, under the occiput. You may feel a special energy there, almost a sense of home. Deepen this feeling and expand it as much as you can. Use the spine as a channel for this feeling, distributing it throughout your body. Expand the feeling so it becomes larger than your body and continues to expand outside your body, on and on.

Do the rotation three or nine times in a clockwise direction. Then find a place in the movement where you feel comfortable changing direction, and begin three or nine counterclockwise rotations. Throughout this movement remember to breathe evenly through both nose and mouth.

On the last rotation, move your head more and more slowly until it finally stops moving. Then sit quietly in the sitting posture for ten minutes, continuing to expand your feelings and energy.

This exercise relieves tension in the neck, head, and shoulders, and lightens the fixed quality of thoughts and images.

Exercise 18　Hand Magic

This exercise is most effective when done after massaging or energizing the hands.

　　Sit cross-legged with your hands on your knees. Slowly lift your arms to chest level, with your elbows bent and your palms down. Relax your elbows and move them away from your body a little. Breathing softly and evenly through both nose and mouth, very slowly move your hands up and down a few inches. Move softly, slowly, and casually, until you feel heat underneath your hands, a slow fire. With your eyes half-closed, use your peripheral vision to look at the motion. Relax your shoulders and move your hands slower and slower, so slowly you can hardly see any movement. Can you feel heat in your palms, at the back of your neck, behind your spinal cord, in your chest?

If you do not feel heat, you may be moving too quickly. Let your hands just hang down from your wrists, and relax your elbows. Move very lightly, as if touching the texture of space. Make the motion smaller, shorter, softer, gentler. Make the movement even slower, until it becomes like a pulsation, almost imperceptible, a tiny bee buzzing softly. Do your palms feel hot? Do you feel something up and down your fingers? Perhaps a tingling with a very special quality?

Once you feel something in your palms or fingers, keep your hands in front of you and slowly turn the palms up, holding them as if they were supporting air. Press your elbows into your sides, and push your chest out a little. Keeping your palms up, slowly move your hands toward each other, feeling the sensations of heat and energy; then before they touch, slowly move them apart, and separate them as much as possible. Can you still feel the energy? Your elbows stay in the same position throughout, firmly pressed into your sides. Continue, three or nine times.

With your palms up and your elbows pressed into your sides, now move your hands toward and away from each other in a very fast, short, strong motion. Relax your belly and let strength pass from your shoulders into your hands. Your neck is straight and strong; your hands shaking as fast as possible. Continue for thirty seconds to one minute.

Gradually slow down the movement of your hands, and allow them to come to rest in your lap, the back of one hand held in the palm of the other, your head bent slightly forward. Relax your shoulders. It is as if your hands encircle the energy and bring it to rest. Sit for five to ten minutes, expanding the sensations in your body. After you have practiced this exercise ten times over a period of a week or two, go on to the following exercises.

☆ Sit cross-legged with your hands on your knees. Breathe gently and evenly through both nose and mouth. Slowly lift your arms to chest level and begin to move your hands in unison in any way you want, feeling the energy inside your palms. Try moving them slowly up and down or from side to side. You may feel sensations of coolness or warmth. Feel the energy in different ways. Perhaps lift your hands as if raising something very heavy like lead, or push down with great strength. You may feel a kind of feeling-form, an energy shape. You may even be able to feel inside the form of the energy.

Now slowly begin to play with the energy. Twist it, pull it, put it together, disperse it, make solid forms—play with it in any way you are moved to do. As you play, let your mind become united with the feelings until there is nothing other than these sensations of energy.

Now grip your sides with your elbows, and with your palms facing each other and the fingers pointing forward, begin to vibrate your hands rapidly back and forth. (Keep the fingers of each hand together.) Start with your hands wide apart, and push the energy together, making it denser and stronger. Let strength come from your shoulders into your hands, so your hands become heavier. Feel the sensations of energy, the different weights and textures. You are contacting air as well as energy; behind the air is the energy. Feel the different qualities of energy—perhaps a quality like fine cloth, or like drinking water.

Now slowly lessen the movement, and bring your hands near (without touching) different places on your body—the top of your head, your throat, your chest, the area below the navel. Move your hands very slowly and feel the different qualities of these energy fields. Then slowly allow your hands to grow still and come to rest on your knees. Sit quietly for several minutes, feeling the energies of this 'hand magic'.

Over a period of several weeks, do this exercise twenty-five times, for ten minutes each session. Then you will become familiar with these different qualities of energy.

☆ When you have done one of the preceding exercises and feel energy in your hands, rub the palms together vigorously and distribute the heat energy generated by this motion to the rest of your body, even to each organ. Rub very fast and strongly with light concentration. Draw your hands up close to your chin and look directly at them as you rub, breathing gently through both nose and mouth. Rub faster and faster, passing the energy into your body.

Now slow the movement down and make it heavier. Slowly cover your eyes with your palms without actually touching the eyes. Feel the energy pass into your eyes. Sit quietly for three to five minutes with your hands over your eyes, feeling the movement of energies within. You may feel sensations in many parts of your body. Let your breath merge with the sensations and amplify them. .

When you release your hands, very slowly open your eyes, and look around in a gentle, open way. Do you notice something different, perhaps a feeling or quality? What is the quality of your breathing?

Exercise 19   Revitalizing Energy

Sit on the floor, not on a mat or cushion, with your legs stretched out in front of you and a comfortable distance apart, your back straight, and your hands on your knees. Flex your ankles so your toes point toward your face, and keep them in this position throughout the movement. Slowly lift your arms in front of you to shoulder height, with the palms down.

Very slowly reach forward toward your toes, lowering your head between your arms. When you have reached as far as you can without straining (it does not matter how far you reach), very, very slowly draw back, keeping your arms stretched out in front of you, and letting your head come up, until you are leaning backwards a little.

Then again reach forward very slowly toward your toes, without straining. Move even more slowly as you draw back, expanding the sensations that arise. Feel the qualities of space and time. Remember to breathe gently and evenly through both nose and mouth throughout the movement.

Do the exercise three or nine times. Then sit in the sitting posture for five to ten minutes, breathing gently and amplifying your sensations until they fill the space around you.

Exercise 20   Touching Body Energy

This exercise is not recommended if you are pregnant
or have had any back or neck injuries.

Stand with your feet a comfortable distance apart,
your back straight, and your body balanced. Breathing softly through both nose and mouth, slowly raise
your arms in front of you until they are overhead,

with the palms facing forward. With your knees relaxed and straight but not locked, slowly bend forward from the waist while reaching out slightly with
your arms. This bending has a quality of arching.
Bend forward and down, very slowly and evenly;
head, torso, and arms move together. Release tension
in your chest, belly, and lower energy centers as you
go down.

Do not let your head dominate the movement; relax your neck muscles so your head hangs freely and
loosely. Feel the sensations in the back of your body,
especially your spine and the backs of your legs. Your
knees are straight. When your fingers come near to the
floor, stay down briefly, concentrating lightly on
your back. Be very still. Slowly spread your fingers
apart more. Exhale fully, releasing tension from your
belly so the flow of energy is not blocked.

Now very slowly, breathing evenly and gently,
begin to rise, keeping your head between your arms.
Bring your attention to your throat as you come up
—you may feel a sensation of opening there. When
you reach an upright position, continue to bend
slightly backward, with your arms quite close to your
head. Move very gently, with your knees straight and
your belly and lower organs relaxed. Bend backward
only a little, without straining. In this position, keep
your exhalations gentle, and let the front of your
body feel open, especially your belly, chest, and
throat.

Slowly straighten your neck and back, bringing
your attention to the base of your skull; perhaps you
will feel warmth there, or a sense of connection and

peace as if you had finally come home. Again bend forward as before, moving as gently and slowly as possible, relaxing your belly, neck, and back. Develop the healing quality of the forward movement, especially in the lower part of your spine. Feel the opening and freeing of the vertebrae. During the first part of the bend, you may be most aware of your upper back. As you bend further, you may feel the middle part of your back opening, and as you approach the floor with your hands, healing energy may be strongest in your lower back.

When you begin to rise, move so slowly and imperceptibly that you can sense the subtle tensions you hold in your body. When you locate a tension, explore it with your feelings as completely as you can. Perhaps you will find an attitude or an aspect of your self-image within the tightness. When you fully experience the tightness, you will then be able to let it go. As you move, become one with your feelings; let them move you, spreading their energy to every molecule in your body until finally 'you' no longer exist, and there is only feeling.

Do the exercise three or nine times. Then sit quietly in the sitting posture for five to ten minutes, expanding the sensations awakened by this movement.

This exercise relieves tension in the back of the neck, the spine, and the backs of the legs, and redistributes energy and feeling throughout the body.

Exercise 21   Healing Body and Mind

Stand with your body well balanced, your feet about
a foot apart, your back straight, and your arms relaxed at your sides. Inhale through both nose and
mouth and slowly lift your arms in front of you until
they are overhead, with the palms facing forward.
While exhaling, slowly bend to the right side, reaching out with your arms and keeping your knees
straight but not locked.

As you bend, let your pelvis move slightly to the left, so your weight is balanced on both feet and the curve on both sides of your body is as long and graceful as possible. Loosen the muscles of your waist, neck, and shoulders, and allow your left hip and the ribs on the left side to open like a fan. Let your left arm come close to your ear, and let your right arm lower a little toward the ground. Keep your mouth slightly open, and let your breath flow evenly.

While inhaling, slowly return to an upright position and in a continuous motion reach to the opposite side while exhaling. Let your belly be relaxed and empty. Move as gradually as you can, feeling the sensations within your body. Do the complete movement, to the right and left, three or nine times, relaxing more each time. Then sit in the sitting posture for five to ten minutes, expanding the feelings stimulated by the exercise. This movement can also be done with the palms facing each other.

This exercise relieves tension in the muscles along the sides of the body.

Exercise 22   Flying

Stand well balanced with your feet about four inches apart, your back straight, and your arms relaxed at your sides. Slowly lift your arms away from your sides until they are directly overhead with the backs of the hands almost touching, and the fingers straight. Close your eyes and feel the sensations of energy in your body. Relax your thighs and minimize any backward arching in your spine. Slowly open your arms, increasing the distance between them in a balanced and equal way, and very gradually let your arms descend to your sides. Take one full minute to bring them all the way down to your sides. Pay attention to the feeling tone as you move, as if seeing with the inner eyes of the senses. Let energy flow into your heart center. You may feel heat and energy surrounding your arms and hands.

Now take another full minute to move your arms up again. Explore the flow of energy: you might try directing energy from your heart center out through your fingers. Use the steady, slow rhythm to increase the energy flow. When your arms are directly overhead, stretch up very slightly, with your thighs and legs as relaxed as possible. This stretch clears and settles the mind; go deeply into your sensations at this point.

Continue the movement nine times. Try slowing the movement down even more, taking two minutes in each direction. To complete the exercise, sit in the sitting posture for five minutes or more, continuing to sense the flow of energy, with breath, body, and mind as one.

This exercise calms the restless flow of thoughts, and generates feeling in the heart center.

Exercise 23   Balancing Body and Mind

Stand barefoot on the floor or ground with your feet a comfortable distance apart and your back straight. Slowly lift your left leg, bending it at the knee. Grasp the inside of the leg near the ankle with your left hand, and place the sole of your left foot, toes down, against the inside of your upper right thigh, with the heel near the crotch. Press the heel lightly into the thigh to hold the leg in position. Move the left knee out to the side, slowly place your hands on your hips, look straight ahead with soft eyes, and balance casually in this position, concentrating lightly. Distribute some of your weight to your left knee, and loosen your belly. Remain in this position for one to three minutes. Without changing position or losing your balance, slowly reduce the pressure of your left foot against your right thigh until it is almost imperceptible.

Now slowly lift your foot from your thigh and lower your leg to the floor, paying special attention to the sensations you feel just before your left foot touches the ground. Slowly resume a standing position balanced on both legs, then repeat the movement on the other side of your body. Notice on which side balance is easier.

Do the complete movement, first one side and then the other, three times. Then sit for ten to fifteen minutes, allowing the sensations stimulated by this posture to expand. See if you can follow the process of coming back to a more familiar state of mind. Do you come back in a balanced way?

If you regularly practice this exercise (or any of the exercises in Part 2 in which you balance on one leg), you will find that different feeling states produce different feeling-tones within balance. You will probably find it more difficult to balance when you are emotional, and tightness in your body may make you lose your balance. Relax into the exercise and go deeply into the feelings awakened within you.

This exercise stretches the upper leg and stimulates energy in the sacrum and spine.

Exercise 24   Being and Body

Stand well balanced with your feet a comfortable
distance apart, your back straight, and your arms
relaxed at your sides. Breathe softly through nose and
mouth. Close your eyes, and let tension ebb from
your entire body, especially your chest and throat.
Take several minutes to sense how tiny adjustments
in muscles and energy affect your balance.

Now slowly open your eyes, look straight ahead, and begin to walk very slowly, taking very small steps, as little as two inches and not more than four. Walk as slowly as you can imagine walking. Then slow down even more.

Each movement of stepping and lifting can be an opportunity for learning. Before lifting each foot, relax your belly and chest. At the moment of stepping, relax your knees, belly, and chest. Relax also your fingers and toes, your skin, even your bones—let every part of your body be calm and warm. Step very lightly and create balance at every moment . . . balance both sides of your body, balance your concentration, balance your breath. You may then discover that your body moves gently by itself.

Between lifting and stepping there is a kind of silence. Tension in the energy centers, especially in the throat center, may block this silent quality. So at the moment of lifting your foot from the ground, relax your throat, as well as your belly, knees, shoulders, hands, and spine. Relax also your way of being aware, so your concentration is not too strong or focused. Then at the crucial point between lifting and stepping, you can be balanced, relaxed, and silent.

Give the same emphasis and the same amount of time to each part of the movement—lifting, moving, stepping. Open your senses in such a way that you do not focus on any particular sense. You are no more aware of seeing than of hearing. Give as much power to your feelings as to your eyes, ears, and thoughts.

Feel as much as you think. Give all aspects of your experience equal weight, letting your body and senses operate as a complete whole. As you walk in this way, be aware of the mantra OM AH HUM. You do not need to actually pronounce it; listen to it inwardly.

Practice this slow walking for forty-five minutes, moving so slowly that you cover ten yards, back and forth, four times. The next time you practice, walk half as slowly, covering ten yards, back and forth, two times in forty-five minutes.

☆ Once you have practiced this slow, balanced walking for three hours, try some variations. Imagine you are working somewhere, perhaps at your office. You want to get home and you are a little late. Close your eyes and feel that feeling: "I have to get home quickly." Now walk with that feeling. How do you move? How does your body feel? Now slow down, and walk very slowly for one minute. Notice any differences in your inner body senses.

Now try another way. Imagine you have to catch a plane—you have an important family engagement, and you *have* to get there quickly. Your mind is extremely busy and rushed, and you want to go faster, but your body moves very, very slowly. Walk, trying to feel equally the anxiety and the slowing down, the very fast and the very slow.

Now intensify the anxiety so you are almost shaking. You want to catch the plane, but you cannot get there. Your mind is extremely agitated because you cannot have what you want. Develop great mental anxiety, a mixture of frustration and pain, almost anger. Slow your walking down even more. Which parts of your body are most tense? Are your hands, chest, and stomach loose? Relax tense places without releasing the strong mental pressure. Can you keep your breathing at an even level?

Now try walking very fast, so your body is rushed, and yet your mind, awareness, and breath are very calm, moving at very slow speed. Your breath and awareness are almost silent. You are not trying either to breathe or to be aware.

Now slow down and walk quietly. Can you equalize the speeds of your body, your breathing, and your awareness? Can your body, breath, and awareness be equally silent and slow, without special emphasis? What is the quality of the energy you feel?

Group Two

At this point in your practice, you have already begun to touch and develop sensations that relax, nurture, and satisfy you. The exercises in this group will help you to deepen these experiences, and will also introduce new feeling-tones which can be extended and enriched.

As you practice, continue to pay attention to the special flavors of feeling each exercise stimulates. Let your body guide you in combining exercises, and in developing sequences of exercises. Do not try to name or label the feeling-tones of your experience; simply feel them. Become acquainted with their qualities: their texture and weight, their sense of time. Although you may not have the vocabulary to describe these subtle feeling-tones, you can experience them.

After spending a few weeks on these exercises, you may feel ready to look at some of the exercises in Part 2. The exercises in Stages One and Two of Part 2 will continue to extend the process of relaxation you have already begun; the exercises in Stage Three will give you an idea of how Kum Nye can be further developed. Be sure, however, not to move too quickly into Part 2, or to try to practice too many exercises at once. Add one or two exercises to the exercises in this group, and develop them fully before going on to more. Then your practice will have a clear, stable quality, and you will develop trust in your experience.

Exercise 25   Calming Inner Energy

Sit cross-legged on a mat or cushion with your back
straight and your hands on your hips. Slowly begin to
move your upper body in a circle. Bend slowly to
your left from the waist, breathing evenly through
both nose and mouth, your head and neck relaxed
and hanging. Then move slowly forward so your
head skims your left knee, passes close to the ground

and then skims your right knee. Move up on the right side, then arch backward slightly, looking toward the ceiling. Without stopping, continue the circle to the left, moving very slowly and maintaining balance. Your mouth should be relaxed and slightly open. Fully exhale in the lower position and breathe normally during the rest of the revolution.

After nine clockwise rotations, slowly change directions and continue for nine counterclockwise rotations. This exercise may bring you to a very still place where you have few or no thoughts. If this happens, slow the movement down even more, expanding this feeling. When you finish the exercise, sit in the sitting posture for five to ten minutes, continuing to follow and extend the sensations stimulated by the movement.

☆ This exercise may also be done standing. Stand well balanced with your hands on your hips, your feet about a foot apart, your knees straight but not locked, and your back straight. Feel a column of energy within your body. Slowly bend forward from your waist, to waist level or a little lower, letting your head hang, and very slowly begin to rotate your upper body in a clockwise circle around the inner column of energy. The revolution should be complete and continuous, although you arch backward much less than you bend forward. Do not strain; relax and let gravity lead you down. Let your belly, neck, shoulders, and jaw be very relaxed. Breathe easily through both nose and mouth.

Very slowly, make three or nine clockwise circles,

then three or nine counterclockwise circles. Concentrate lightly on the sensations traveling down your spine as you move; feel them more. Broaden your concentration to encompass the pelvis as well—light concentration here will help to support your body and increase the flow of energy. Feel the balancing of the inner column. When you finish the rotations, sit in the sitting posture for five to ten minutes, exploring the sensations stimulated by this movement.

☆ Another version of this exercise is as follows: stand well balanced with your feet about a foot apart, and your arms relaxed at your sides. Slowly lift your arms away from your sides until they are overhead, and turn the palms to face each other. Imagine that your hands are carrying a large ball of energy. In this position, continuing to imagine the ball of energy carried in your hands, bend forward at the waist to about waist level, and begin to rotate your upper body slowly in a clockwise circle. Breathe easily through both nose and mouth, concentrating lightly on your pelvis and the sensations moving down your spine.

Feel energy flowing from the ball of energy through your hands, arms, and head, passing down your spine. Become the ball of energy moving silently through space. Make three or nine very slow clockwise circles, then three or nine very slow counterclockwise circles. To complete the exercise, sit in the sitting posture for five to ten minutes, expanding the feelings within and around your body.

These exercises calm the internal organs and the nervous system.

Exercise 26   Stimulating Inner Energy

Sit cross-legged on a mat or cushion with your back
straight and your hands on your knees. Bring your
attention to your navel area, and slowly begin to
move your belly in a circle, up on the right and down
on the left. Do the movement very slowly, going
deeply into the sensations stimulated by it. Notice
that as your belly makes a circle, your chest also
moves in a circle.

Breathe softly through both nose and mouth, and let the slow circling movement of your belly and chest become fuller and deeper, so the movement massages all your internal organs as well as the sides of your body. Continue for several minutes, until the feeling of the massage becomes almost tangible. Try a few circles in the other direction.

Now slow the movement down even more, so that the massage is stimulated more by feeling-tone than by movement. Let body, breath, and mind become one. Then gradually let the movement lessen until you finally stop moving. Sit quietly and let the massage of feeling permeate every part of your body and continue for as long as possible. The longer the feeling-tone is expanded, the more the massage moves beyond the body, stimulating interactions with the surrounding universe.

When the feeling-tone begins to fade, experiment with ways to stimulate the belly and chest massage without moving physically. Try turning the belly around like a ball with the breath. Also try moving the belly up and down with the breath. Then activate the massage with concentration only, as if the senses were rubbing themselves internally.

Exercise 27   Touching Nurturing Feeling

Sit comfortably on a mat or cushion in a cross-legged position, with your knees wide apart, and your back straight. Place your hands on the top of your upper thighs, with the fingers pointing forward. In this position, slowly push your hands against your thighs so your arms straighten and both shoulders are lifted as high as possible. When you think your shoulders are as high as they can be, relax your body, and you may find your shoulders can move up a little more. Settle your neck down between your shoulders; your chin will almost touch your chest. Breathe lightly through both nose and mouth, with your throat and belly as relaxed as possible. Hold this posture for three to five minutes (you can measure the time by counting outbreaths), raising energy from the belly area into your chest. Keep the energy high, 'holding' it in a balanced way.

After three to five minutes, very slowly loosen your shoulders a little. Do not rotate your shoulders as they loosen; simply release the tension little by little, and allow your shoulders to move down in the same vertical plane. Your elbows will bend as your arms relax. Take at least one minute for the release. Feel energy flowing down the length of your spine, from the neck to the lower back and sacrum. When you first do this exercise, the energy will flow down the spine, then forward and up inside your body to the throat, then back and down the spine. Later you will be able to move the energy in every direction, to all parts of your body.

Now modify the exercise slightly. Push your hands against your thighs, straighten your elbows, and lift your shoulders as before, but this time make your belly a little smaller, and tighten the back of your spine slightly. It may seem that you are trying to control your breath, but instead just breathe slowly through both nose and mouth. Be very still and hold this position for three to five minutes. If you feel a little pain in your neck, upper shoulders, or lower back, slowly move your shoulders slightly so energy can flow smoothly there.

After three to five minutes, very slowly relax the tension and feel the deep, sensitive feeling that arises. Let the tension go completely from your arms in a natural way—very gradually and slowly. Take your time. You may feel warmth in your chest and the back of your neck or a sensation of opening in your chest, throat, and head, a feeling of expanding beyond your body. Do the exercise three or nine times. Be as relaxed and open as possible, not holding back, not specifically focused on anything.

To complete the exercise, sit in the sitting posture for ten to fifteen minutes, expanding the sensations generated by holding and releasing tension in this way.

This exercise stretches the muscles and ligaments between the bones of the upper body, especially the upper spine, and circulates energy to the spine and joints. It can also be done standing.

Exercise 28   Body of Knowledge

If you have had any kind of back or neck injury or
have had an operation within three or four months,
move carefully in this exercise and do less than the
directions indicate.

Sit cross-legged on a mat or cushion, making sure
that your pelvis is higher than your legs. Place your
hands on your knees so the fingers point towards

each other, with the fingers and thumb of each hand together. The elbows point out to the side. Slowly arch your head forward and down so your chin moves toward your chest.

In this position, bend forward from the waist as slowly as you can, pressing your hands firmly against your knees, and pushing your elbows forward a little. Gently pull your belly back against your spine and hold it tightly, breathing softly and evenly through both nose and mouth.

Each time you exhale, let each section of your spine—between your shoulder blades, the middle back, the lower back, at the sacrum—open and expand. You may feel as if space opens between each vertebra, and even within each spinal bone. When you have bent forward as far as you can without straining, focus lightly on the base of your spine; you may feel an opening there, and a sensation of warmth.

Expand these feelings as much as you can, up your spine and throughout your body. Stay down for three to five minutes. (You can measure the time by counting outbreaths.)

Just before you begin to come up, change your hand position so the fingers and thumbs point straight ahead. As you come up, press your hands strongly against your legs. The tension may cause mild shaking; stay with the shaking and notice what you feel. You may move beyond the shaking to a plateau where the shaking continues but your breath becomes tranquil and soft. At that point your mind has a crystal quality.

Very slowly release the tension and sit quietly for five minutes, expanding the feelings stimulated by the exercise. Do the movement three or nine times, sitting for five minutes after each repetition. To complete the exercise, sit for ten to fifteen minutes, continuing to expand the sensations within and around your body.

To develop this exercise further, stay down for longer periods of time, up to twenty minutes (in such a case, do it only once), and sit afterward for the same length of time you stay down.

This exercise relieves eyestrain and general tiredness. It also helps to build muscles, and to improve the functioning of the joints.

☆ This variation of the above exercise is a little more difficult. Sit on a mat or cushion with your legs loosely crossed. The position of your legs will affect your balance in doing this exercise, so you may want to experiment with different ways of crossing them until you find the position that permits the most balanced movement.

Interlace your fingers and place them on the back of your neck, keeping your elbows out. Slowly push your neck down with your hands so your chin moves toward your chest. In this position, bend forward slowly from the waist, breathing lightly and evenly through both nose and mouth, with your belly held tightly against your spine. As you exhale, let each part of your spine open and expand. When you have bent forward as far as you can without straining, focus lightly on the base of your spine, allowing the sensations there to spread out like a halo.

Then, without holding the position, come up as slowly as you can. As your spine straightens, hold some strength in the muscles of your chest, as if directing an energy flow through your chest up into your throat. Then slowly lower your hands to your knees and sit for a few minutes, breathing gently and evenly through both nose and mouth.

Do this exercise three or nine times, sitting briefly after each repetition. At the end, sit for five to ten minutes, continuing to expand the sensations at the base of your spine, and in your chest and throat, until they are distributed throughout your body and become part of the space that surrounds you. Let the feelings spread out like a mandala.

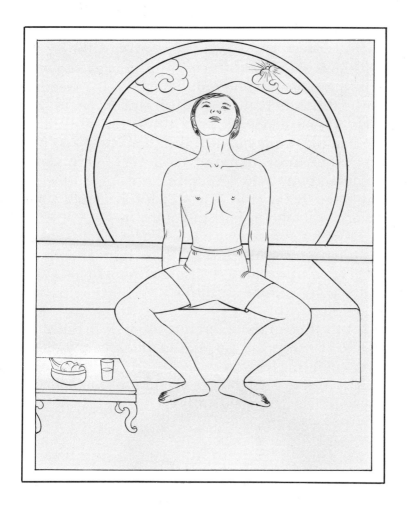

Exercise 29   Clear Light

Do this exercise very gently if you are pregnant, if you have had any sort of back or neck injury, or if you have had an operation within three or four months.

Sit on the edge of a straight chair with your feet flat on the floor about six inches apart, the heels pointing toward each other, and the toes pointing out. Place your hands in back of you on the chair with the fingers pointing behind you. Breathing lightly through both nose and mouth, press your hands down, and arch your spine and neck backward, letting your mouth fall open. Hold for thirty seconds to three minutes; then very, very slowly straighten your neck and back, sensing the feelings stimulated by the arch. You may feel heat in the back of your neck and the base of your spine.

Sit with your hands on your knees for a few minutes, distributing these sensations throughout your body. Then repeat the exercise two more times, sitting for five to ten minutes at the end.

A variation of this exercise is done with the hands next to the hips on the side of the chair, with the fingers pointing forward.

This exercise can relieve ulcers and stomach pain, as well as psychological tensions.

Exercise 30   Expanding Awareness

Sit cross-legged on a mat or cushion, and place your
hands in your lap with the palms up, the right hand
held in the left. Loosen your belly and chest, settle
your neck down between your shoulders, and relax
tension in your spine. Gracefully lift your arms
overhead, finishing with the palms facing forward.
Imagine a huge ball of energy in front of you. Slowly

open your arms and move them down in lateral arcs as if encircling this ball of energy with your hands. Feel the sensations of energy in your hands and arms.

As you round the bottom of the ball, with your palms up, cross the right wrist over the left without touching them together, and in a continuing movement, twist both wrists until the palms face away from you. Keeping your hands in the same plane, draw them toward each other slightly. Without ceasing the movement, slowly and gracefully lift your arms in front of you, first your right arm, and as soon as there is enough room, your left arm, keeping your elbows and hands relaxed. Move your arms up in a balanced way until they are both outstretched overhead, and the movement, with its special design, has begun again.

Do the movement three or nine continuous times. With each repetition, relax more deeply, allowing the sensations awakened by the movement to spread throughout your body. Breathe very softly through both nose and mouth, with your belly and chest relaxed. Then adapt the 'rounding the ball' movement to bring your hands to rest on your knees. Sit for five to ten minutes, continuing to expand the sensations of energy within and outside of your body.

This exercise expands awareness and concentration, and releases tension in the upper back and shoulders. Try it after sitting for fifteen to thirty minutes.

Exercise 31 Knowing Only Bliss

Kneel on a rug or on the ground with your thighs
vertical. Lift your right knee and place your right foot
on the floor, with the toes a few inches to the right of
your left knee. Sit back on your left heel and bring
your right heel to the floor. (You will keep your right
foot flat on the floor throughout the movement.) Place
your palms flat on the floor, the left palm a few inches

to the left of the left knee, and the right palm a few inches to the right of the right foot, so the hands, knee, and foot are in a line. Now lower your head and lift your pelvis so you can stand on the toes of your left foot. Be alert and sensitive to these toes during the exercise, so you do not put too much weight on them.

In this position, keeping your palms flat on the floor, lift your chest as much as possible, and look up toward the ceiling. Hold for fifteen to thirty seconds, breathing gently through both nose and mouth, and concentrating lightly on your back. Then slowly lower your head and let it hang loosely. Now lift your pelvis slightly and strongly press both hands, your left knee and your right foot to the ground. Hold for fifteen to thirty seconds, breathing easily through both nose and mouth. Slowly release the tension, straighten your left foot, and sit in the sitting posture for a few minutes.

Now reverse the position of the legs and repeat the exercise. Do the complete movement, first on one side, then on the other, three times, resting briefly after each repetition. At the end, sit quietly for five to ten minutes, expanding the sensations stimulated within and around you.

This exercise relieves tension in the neck and stimulates energy in the lower back which then flows up the back and through the neck.

Exercise 32   Touching Body, Mind, and Energy

Stand well balanced with your feet a comfortable distance apart, your back straight, and your arms relaxed at your sides. Slowly raise your arms in front of you to a little above shoulder height, with your hands about two inches apart, the backs of the hands facing each other and the fingers straight. Picture steel bars next to your palms and begin to move your arms slowly out to the sides, as if you were pushing these steel bars apart. Push with strength until your outstretched arms are a little behind your shoulders. Breathe lightly and evenly through both nose and mouth. Keep your belly, chest, and thighs relaxed and concentrate lightly on the base of the spine. If you feel painful tenseness in the muscles of your upper and middle back, move more gently.

Now imagine that the steel bars are near the backs of your hands, and slowly move your hands toward the front, as if you were pushing the bars together. Notice the different quality of the movement in this direction. Feel the energy surrounding your hands and arms, while still concentrating loosely on the base of the spine.

Release the tension in your arms very slowly, and lower them to your sides. Stand for two minutes, expanding the sensations of energy. Then continue the exercise, three or nine times, standing with your arms at your sides after each repetition. When you finish, sit for five minutes or more, sensing the energy flow in your body.

This exercise increases circulation and awareness, and will invigorate you when you feel tired, sleepy, or clumsy.

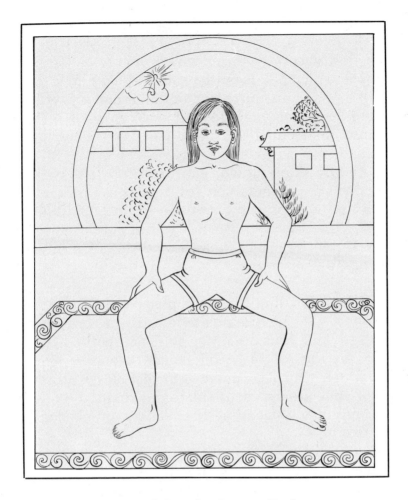

Exercise 33 Energizing the Lower Body

Stand well balanced with your back straight, your
legs wide apart, and your toes turned out slightly. Place your hands on your thighs, with your thumbs
toward the inside of the leg. Breathe softly through
both nose and mouth; relax your shoulders, and look
straight ahead with your back straight. In this
position, bend your knees and lower your pelvis until

you find a certain place where energy is strongly activated in your legs (they may shake). You may need to move up and down a little or move your legs closer or wider apart to find it. Keep your weight evenly distributed on both feet, and your back straight.

As you move down, you may find that tension somewhere prevents you from moving further. Locate the tension, gently release it, and continue to lower. Use the exercise to explore subtle tensions which interfere with balance and the even flow of energy in your body.

When you find the right place, hold for fifteen seconds, with your genital and anal areas open and relaxed, and your breathing soft. You will feel pressure on the knees. After fifteen seconds, slowly straighten your legs, move your feet closer together, relax your arms at your sides, and stand or sit for a few minutes, expanding the feelings quickened by the exercise.

Do the exercise three times, resting after each repetition; then sit in the sitting posture for five to ten minutes, continuing to amplify and extend the sensations in your body. As you become more familiar with this exercise, try holding the position for longer periods of time. Also try inhaling as you move down, and exhaling as you come up.

This exercise releases energy blockages in the lower body.

Exercise 34   Inner Gold

Stand well balanced with your feet about six inches
apart and your back straight. Interlace your fingers
and place them at the back of your neck, so they
support your head. Slowly push your neck back
against your hands, spread your elbows apart as wide
as possible, bend your knees slightly, and lift your
chest toward the ceiling. The lower part of your spine

should be as relaxed as possible, while your upper spine arches backwards. In this position, exhale very slowly and deeply for as long as you can. Feel the stretch in the muscles under your arms and at the sides of your chest. Go deeply into the sensations that arise in your chest.

Now, while inhaling, slowly and steadily press your hands against the back of your neck, bending your neck forward and lowering your elbows until your chin is near your chest, and your elbows hang down close together. As you reach this lowered position, hold your breath a tiny bit, and relax the muscles of your shoulders and upper back. Then continuing to inhale, slowly push your neck against your hands, move your elbows wide apart, and lift your chest toward the ceiling, allowing it to open. Exhale in the open position.

Continue this opening and folding movement three or nine times, as slowly as can be coordinated with your breathing. Then sit in the sitting posture for ten minutes, expanding the sensations stimulated by the exercise.

As you experience more openness physically in the heart area, you may feel a deep, open, loving feeling which can be distributed to all parts of your body, and expanded beyond your body to the surrounding universe. This exercise also relieves pain and tension in the stomach area.

Other Dharma Publishing Books

Time, Space, and Knowledge: A New Vision of Reality by Tarthang Tulku. Thirty-five exercises and a rigorous philosophical text reveal new horizons of knowledge, unique in their richness and depth.

Gesture of Balance by Tarthang Tulku. The Nyingma method of meditation wherein all life experience is meditation.

Openness Mind by Tarthang Tulku. The sequel to *Gesture of Balance*, with more advanced meditation techniques.

Skillful Means by Tarthang Tulku. A manual for making work a source of unlimited fulfillment.

Kindly Bent to Ease Us by Longchenpa. A translation of Longchenpa's guide to the Dzogchen path to enlightenment.

The Life and Liberation of Padmasambhava by Yeshe Tsogyal. A translation of the complete biography of Tibetan Buddhism's founder. Two volumes, 58 color plates.

Crystal Mirror Series edited by Tarthang Tulku. Introductory explorations of the various aspects of Tibetan philosophy, history, psychology, art, and culture. Five volumes currently available.

Calm and Clear by Lama Mipham. Translations of two beginning meditation texts by a brilliant 19th century Tibetan Lama.

If you order Dharma books directly from the publisher, it will help us to make more such books available. Write for a free catalog and new book announcements.

Dharma Publishing   2425 Hillside Avenue
Berkeley, California 94704   USA